The Path to Joy

Tom Clem
4/13/22

The Path to Joy

Navigating the Stages of Faith

Tom Clements

First printed 2021

Copyright © 2021 by Tom Clements
All rights reserved.

Clements, Tom
The Path to Joy: Navigating the Stages of Faith

ISBN: 978-0-578-30742-8

www.thepath2joy.com

This book is dedicated to each of the spiritual directors that I have had in my life—Sister Barbara, Father Peter, Father David, Father Michael and Father Kevin. I appreciate your coaching, encouragement, faith, persistence, and example, as you helped me to grow closer to God. You had a difficult challenge! I cannot thank you enough for your gift of self to me in my faith journey.

CONTENTS

PREFACE

This book was written for you. You picked it up because something tugged at you. This tug led to a desire to know more which, in turn, led you onto your faith journey. The goal of this book is to help you visualize the "whole path" of your faith journey in clear, practical stages. Then, you can use that understanding to determine where you are on that path, and what you can do next to go deeper into your faith. And because I am a frustrated comedian, I will attempt to throw in some humor as you navigate each stage.

One of the biggest myths out there is that religious people are dour, super-serious and strange. Television shows and movies love to reinforce that stereotype. During my own faith journey, I was fearful that if I committed myself to God, I would become one of "those" people. I have been blessed through my journey to have run into a completely different group of people who are great fun, high achievers and just regular folk, putting to bed that myth. What a pleasure to realize that you can be fun AND have a great faith life. The relief I felt in meeting deeply religious, God-fearing men and women who laugh, hike, read and play, motivated me to stay the course. For instance, I met a man who was a National Collegiate Athletic Association (NCAA) athlete, a lover of nature, a professor of Shakespeare and who seemed to know every mascot for every college team in the country. He was a man's man, and for a time while we worked together, we walked with each other to Christ. It truly motivated me.

I hope to more clearly present the stages with some examples of my joy of God. I share my struggles and successes as I continue to traverse these stages. Knowing the stages does not mean that presto, you made the change. One of my favorite sayings is: "Reading a book on baseball does not mean you can hit a 95-mile-per-hour fastball!" Nonetheless, I hope knowing what is involved at each step helps you visualize where you are in the process, and understand some actions you might take to get closer to God. This isn't a stand-alone text. You also have the beauty and tools of the Catholic Church at your disposal. You might choose to explore, discuss and experience life in order to move forward. But, with effort, you will get closer to God. I wish I'd had something like this available to me as a beginner, or even as an intermediate person, on my faith journey.

In writing this, I was trying to figure out two things: 1) What are the stages that I have taken in my faith journey, and where do I go next? And, 2) How do I work with others to help them get closer to Christ? On this second point, everyone I talk to says you have to meet people where they are. Well, where are they? How do I tell? So, I developed this guide for my personal use, but shared it with several people. It spread pretty rapidly with people calling or emailing me comments and questions. I realized I had hit on an area where there is not a lot of practical information for today's world.

I am not developing any new concepts or beliefs, no new prayers or means of sanctification. It is my intention that every point is consistent with the precepts of the Catholic Church. It is funny. I once heard some prayers that I assumed had been made up by members of an order of priests with whom I had been working. I was a little put off that we were saying these non-standard prayers! Imagine my surprise when I found out that the prayers were posted in hymnals and prayer books. They were standard Catholic prayers that I didn't know existed, that's all. I not only found that reassuring, but beautiful. We have available to us so many "tried and tested" ways to get closer to God. We can choose means based on our temperament, station in life or where we are in our faith journey.

Finally, I use the following quote from St. Francis De Sales as my introduction. "One thing more, dear reader. It is too true that I who write about the devout life am not myself devout, but most certainly I am not without the wish to become so, and it is this wish which encourages me to teach you."[1]

I hope that you enjoy the book, learn several nuggets of wisdom from it and use it both for your own journey and for reaching out to others. Please feel free to reach out to me at Tom.thepath2joy@gmail.com. I would like to hear from you.

THE GOAL: JOY

W hy are you reading this book? Perhaps you feel something is missing in your life, or you want more of the little something you have experienced now and then. And what is that? Joy.

Jesus said, "The kingdom of God is within you."[1]

That's a pretty awesome statement. I mean, trust me, I have looked high and low for fulfillment, and to find it not "out there" but "in here" is pretty incredible. It means that you can control whether you are joyful or not. There are many points throughout scripture that allude to this, but I like this explicit statement from someone experiencing joy, King David. In his sixteenth psalm he writes, "You make known to me the path of life; in your presence there is fullness of joy; at your right hand are pleasures forevermore."[2]

This is a book about growing your faith to the point of being joyful. I am convinced that no matter your place in the world, no matter your situation in life, you can be joyful. I don't mean jumping up and down with momentary happiness, but feeling a deep serenity and warmth that you are in sync with God.

The starting point for a life of faith, funnily enough, may require some questioning of the existence of God. "Does God exist?" is a question that almost all of us have asked. Or, your position might even be that

God does not exist. In that case, congratulations, you have belief! I.e. you believe that God doesn't exist. You are on your way.

Seriously, once you desire to know the answer to that question or that position, you are a little closer on the path to cultivating a deep relationship with God. You can start there and challenge those beliefs. You become a seeker. This is something you will most likely be for the rest of your life!

We have choices. We can either meander aimlessly through life or we can try to discern our own path. My experience is that those who don't plan, and instead let things happen to them, seem destined to fail. Too often I have heard a child, a friend, even an acquaintance explain a situation and lament, "why do these things always happen to me?" Often, it is a lack of action early on in the process that laid the groundwork for the "train wreck".

For them, and for all of us, the task is to answer the questions, "What do you want out of life?" "What do you aspire to?" and "How are you going to achieve those goals?"

I think for many of us the answer is "we want to be happy". We might try to do that by making a ton of money, having a great marriage, or by living a life of service to others.

So, what's wrong with pursuing happiness? Well, it depends what we mean by happiness. I am going to simplify a concept—and the linguists reading this might howl—and parse the word happiness into three separate terms: pleasure, happiness, and joy. The definition of each is:

Pleasure is a bodily feeling. It is an emotional response to a sensory experience, contentment, or good fortune. I eat chocolate, I am happy. I get drunk, I am mellow. I play video games, I am excited. Often when the experience ends, so does the pleasure.

HAPPINESS IS the mental state of well-being and contentment. Happiness can be attained by indulging in enjoyable pastimes such as being at the beach, feeling pride in an accomplishment or achievement, or simply by doing something good for others. While the experience of pleasure may contribute to happiness, it is the mental understanding of that which creates the pleasure that helps cultivate a state of happiness. Happiness then, is transitory.

The most superior form of happiness is joy. "**Joy** is a state of mind and an orientation of the heart. It is a settled state of contentment, confidence and hope."[3]

Unfortunately, many of those who say they are generally happy feel they still are not fulfilled. They are not satisfied. They do not have joy.,

So what does satisfy? Achieving the purpose for which you were created. St. John Paul II said it best: "It is Jesus that you seek when you dream of happiness; He is waiting for you when nothing else you find satisfies you; He is the beauty to which you are so attracted; it is He who provoked you with that thirst for fullness that will not let you settle for compromise; it is He who urges you to shed the masks of a false life; it is He who reads in your heart your most genuine choices, the choices that others try to stifle.

It is Jesus who stirs in you the desire to do something great with your lives, the will to follow an ideal, the refusal to allow yourselves to be ground down by mediocrity, the courage to commit yourselves humbly and patiently to improving yourselves and society, making the world more human and more fraternal."[4]

While most of us are just trying to discern what our relationship with God is and how we might go deeper, others might say that this is what they have been trying to do. "Seek first the kingdom of God and his righteousness, and all these things will be added to you.[5] So, why are we not joyful? The short answer is, we have too many attachments to earthly things and we have not given God control. The rest of this book is dedicated to helping you get to that point, without fear. The purpose of this book is to meet you where YOU are on YOUR faith journey and help you grow in your faith to the point of being joyful.

I believe being joyful, while not necessary continuous, is a sustainable state. In many stories of their martyrdom, saints were always joyful on their way to their death. Imagine the following. Here are two such quotes, the first written by the martyr herself in her diary, the day before her death:

Saint Perpetua said: "Then Hilarianus passed sentence on all of us: we were condemned to the beasts, and we returned to prison in high spirits."

Come on. You just got sentenced to death and you write that you were in high spirits? The editor of St. Perpetua's letters concludes the story after her death:

"The day of their victory dawned, and they marched from the prison to the amphitheater joyfully as though they were going to heaven, with calm faces, trembling, if at all, with joy rather than fear. Perpetua went along with shining countenance and calm step, as the beloved of God, as a wife of Christ, putting down everyone's stare by her own intense gaze."[6]

Saint Lawrence: "[The Emperor] had a great gridiron prepared with coals beneath it, and had Lawrence's body placed on it. After the martyr had suffered the pain for a long time, the legend concludes, he made his famous cheerful remark, 'It is well done. Turn me over!'"[7]

How can this be? Making jokes while being burnt alive? Or, like Perpetua, his love of God was so strong he KNEW that by being in complete or intimate communion with God, God would protect him. In both cases, these people died. God did not take away their pain. They had so much love that it enabled their faith and trust in God to bring them everlasting joy in heaven.

I used to feel that the good thief, (i.e. the thief on the cross next to Jesus to whom Jesus said, "today you will be with Me in Paradise"[8]), was the luckiest person in the world. See, he was able to live his life however he wanted to and still got to go to heaven. But then I thought about that. I mean, he DID die on a cross. And, most likely, he was not joyful in life. I believe that not only can you be joyful in this life, but this orientation is what conditions you for eternal life.

I now believe that the kingdom of God is among us. Many negative things will still happen to you, but your attitude toward these things will change, and you will be prepared, as best as one can be, for heaven. On earth, which is not heaven, you can "have life and have it more abundantly."[9]

This is not going to be easy. You will be at war with yourself. (I noticed that I personally put up a pretty good fight against growing closer to God.) Some things will seem intuitively backward. It may take years, if not decades. Nonetheless, the best time to start is today.

What are you aiming for? Short term pleasure, occasional happiness, or life-transforming joy?

You may not feel like "Lov[ing] God with all your heart, all your soul, all your will and all your strength"[10]. I get that. You don't walk up to a stranger and say, "boy, I really love you." Loving God requires having a relationship. It takes time. It takes intentional action. But anyone can get there.

Are you searching? Are you currently depressed? Is your marriage a shambles? Are you caught up in addiction or some other sinful behavior? Or do you just feel "meh"? You can become joyful. How do I know? I have been there and I have seen others who have been there also reach the pinnacle. I was very unhappy. I had talked to my wife about divorce, I had no pleasure or sense of fulfillment in my work or faith and I looked for happiness in the vanities of this world.

I made a choice to seek God, and one choice became another choice, and over a good many years, I am standing in the doorway to joy. Oh, there were consequences of my previous behavior, and most likely, there will be for you too. But, if you pray to God to forgive you, and ask Him to help you, and you make the commitment, you WILL be joyful.

I BELIEVE IN GOD
Stage One

I t starts with a choice. What is your world view?

There are two main world views: 1. God exists and created the world and all of the people, and; 2. God does not exist, never did and we are all on our own.

In the 'God does not exist' world view, man is a result of cosmic chance. Therefore, there really isn't any inherent purpose to life. If this is your world view, you may want to be a good person, and they are many people in this category. They create their own framework of right and wrong. They feel good when they do nice things for others and they want to be perceived in a certain way. They may feel some responsibility for making the world a better place, but that isn't a universal reality, just their opinion. In fact, how can it be true for everyone if life is random? "Truth" then, is a function of votes and peoples' feelings towards things. Issues like abortion and slavery may be wrong in one millennium but okay in another, as that generation becomes more "enlightened".

In the 'God exists' world view, you owe your existence to God. You did nothing to deserve your birth, your innate skills or your circumstances. These free gifts cause anyone who is appreciative to feel grateful. That gratitude also contributes towards a sense of responsibility.

Believing in God is the first stage of faith. If God exists, then you have at least a belief that something outside of you created you. You may choose to be self-absorbed and not think about it, but He is there.

The challenge is to become more aware of the gifts you have been given. Whether you choose to honor that awareness through prayer, contemplation, talking to others or even by going through tough experiences, you can appreciate how fortunate you are. You still might compare yourself to others who have more. You still may complain about your difficulties or even say "why me?" But there is a spark of understanding that you have been given much, regardless of what others have.

When you are successful in fully appreciating God's generosity, you feel compelled to give thanks and live a life worthy of that gift. While you still strive to be happy, you orient yourself to use your talents for the greater glory of God, which providentially, makes you happy! The deeper you go into your faith, the more joyful you become. Don't believe me? Read the rest of the book!

Gratitude

I believe gratitude is the difference-maker in one's life. If you believe God created and maintains the world, that he gave you your life, your skills and your ability to love, to have relationships and to experience the goodness of the earth, then internalizing that to recognize that EVERYTHING that you have is a gift, changes the way you look at things, i.e. your world view.

I can hear you saying, "Great, I get that. How do I become more grateful?"

You need to recognize the gift to appreciate it. Therefore, contemplation and prayer are key methods of discerning the many blessings in your life.

I heard a great line once that applies here: "I used to think that I hit a home run until I realized I was born on third base." Hopefully, you can start to realize the gifts that you receive in many of the daily activities that you do each day.

Even your weaknesses are gifts! I am a careless person. You might say, "well, just be more careful." Ha. I have tried to be but I have a very short attention span and also have many ideas in my head at the same time. Even though I try, I often spill food and drink on the table, floor or my clothes. I do not like that about myself and it's humiliating.

Yet, I truly thank God for this "gift" that keeps me from being so prideful. It gives me empathy in my marriage, or in my relationships or encounters with others when I see what I perceive as a flaw in someone. Often, when judging them, I say to myself, "Yes, what about you, Tom?" This simple flaw keeps me in check.

"Tom, you don't understand; my situation is different."

Yes, you are correct. I don't know your situation. I would never want to minimize or dismiss your suffering or the injustices you may have experienced. But, I do want to share the results of my experience of shifting my attitude towards gratitude. When I look back on the difficult moments of my life, I can't help but be amazed at how God has drawn so much goodness from them in such a way that I would never have predicted or foreseen.

I do know people who are joyful in spite of severe circumstances: A woman who has been confined to a wheelchair for years with multiple sclerosis, a man who has suffered from depression for many years, and a young man who lost years of his life due to addiction. Rather than developing a victim mentality, or behaving spitefully towards others, they are living their lives to the fullest. Why? Because they have the joy of Christ in their heart.

I might not understand your specific situation, but I do know suffering. My son once had a horrible car accident and was in a coma for weeks, and it was doubtful that he would live. (He is now married with four children!) I once got fired from a job while I was supporting a stay-at-home wife and four small children after we had recently moved to a distant city. My wife and I once contemplated divorce. These are just some of the things that happened before I was forty!

Thankfully, today, my wife Julie and I are happy and in love. She is my best friend. Oh, we struggle with our own happiness—we are human. We even bicker occasionally, but then I always apologize (wink).

My thoughts about Julie went from, "she isn't fulfilling me" to "she has some incredible talents that I am in awe of". A feeling of "poor me" became "I am so blessed".

What changed? My attitude. I went from being 'Tom at the center of the universe' (well, most of the time) to appreciating some of the gifts I had been given—the ability to breathe, to see beauty in sceneries, art and people, to laugh, and to appreciate so many other joys in being alive. Now, please, this book isn't meant to be about me per se, and trust me, I sin often and struggle every day. I am prideful and self-centered, but I am grateful and joyful in knowing that God loves me. He loves you too!

Reflection

1. What is your world view?
2. Do you say either "why do bad things always happen to me?" or "I am so blessed"?
3. Come up with 100 things (yes, 100) for which you are grateful. If you can't come up with 100, go ask your spouse or a friend.
4. What have you done to deserve those 100 things? What gifts have you been given that have allowed you to realize some success?
5. To whom do you feel grateful?

SEEKING GOD
Stage Two

I believe in God. This is an easy statement to say. There is no explanation or logical argument justifying its position. "I got the God thing covered." Just a declaration. Something like, "I believe that Toad the Wet Sprocket is the best band of all time." Why? "They just are!"

Like many people, you might feel a void in your life. You don't know what it is or why you have it, but you don't want to feel that emptiness. You try to be upbeat and positive but you still are not content. You desire a purpose which provides direction and meaning. Socrates said, "An unexamined life isn't worth living."[1] In other words, if you don't question your existence and its purpose, you are doomed to meander through life. As St. Augustine said, "Our heart is restless until it rests in thee."[2]

But, are you looking for God or are you just looking to ease your pain or find happiness? As you search, God may not be the solution you are looking for. Some of us spend years, as Johnny Lee sang many years ago, "Looking for love in all the wrong places."

Many people spend a good part of their lives, if not all of their lives, spinning their wheels. Conflicted because life is not what they want it to be. Their sentiment is often either, "I am afraid to give up my pleasures" or "I don't want to lose control." If you have that attitude, the problem is you currently are not pleased (because earthly pleasures don't truly satisfy) and you don't have any control!

We all realize, some sooner than others, that obtaining the dream job, developing excellence in a sport or extracurricular activity, or marrying a certain person, didn't fulfill us, except possibly for a short time.

It is easy to understand why many of us have doubts and feel confused about God's role in our lives, let alone have belief that He is what fills the emptiness. War, violence against others, famine and other natural disasters all beg the question, "Why?"

The answer to this question has had a great deal written about it. I will attempt to summarize the topic without simplifying the significance out of my answer.

Man is an imperfect creature by design. We are made to be in communion with God. By virtue of gratitude and God's grace, we recognize our dependence and need for God. This allows us to get outside of our self-orientation and to love God and love our fellow man. The full expression of this is what heaven will be. God created us not to be slaves but to freely choose Him. In using our free will, we may choose what is not best for us. Adding to this our inclination to sin, we often chose to not include God in our lives.

The world is not heaven. Nonetheless, we try to eliminate suffering in our lives. While we have made many advancements in science, medicine, and even psychotherapy, our world and mankind are still very flawed. We are not self-sustainable and many things happen outside of our control.

We learn often from trial and error. We know from our own experience that we learn more from our failures than our successes. Often, it takes a long time to convert to a new position and fully embrace the Truth. We are given a lifetime to choose God.

Ok, but why did God make it so messy? Why do there have to be so many steps? I resolved this dilemma for myself using two arguments: One, if God made everything clear and all I had to do was read the Truth, would I accept it? I have concluded that most likely I would have fought it. The bible backs this up with examples of God speaking to people directly and they still did not believe, or if they believed, it was for only a while and they did not stay committed. As an example, when Jesus gave the Bread of Life discourse , He told the people that He was from the Father, that He was the way to heaven. He was direct. He told them straight up. Yet, many people responded with, "'This saying is hard; who can accept it?'...As a result of this, many [of] his disciples returned to their former way of life and no longer accompanied him."[3] This makes it easier for me to accept the second argument, that God is perfect and this must be the most efficacious way for us to learn, believe and to choose Him.

And so, to find God, you must look for Him. You may want to be open to the fact that God just might be the solution to your longing. To become open, you might try to look at things from a different perspective. And that is challenging when we are so self-focused.

A much-needed quality for personal growth—spiritual or otherwise—is objectivity. If you perceive things as they are, you can make the appropriate action or change. You want to honestly look at yourself and your resources and evaluate your own response to what life brings you.

You have chosen to believe in God. You want to be happy and fulfilled. What does that really mean to you and how will you choose to live your life based on that commitment? **Stage two is about making the decision to search for God, and not just believe in Him.**

Humility is a key ingredient to a relationship with God. Can you find God without humility? Of course you can. I did, to a degree. It just makes the road a lot longer as you are measuring so many things incorrectly and giving yourself credit where it isn't due.

Humility

I sometimes tell people I am the most humble person I know! I find that funny on several levels but mostly I tell them I am so humble because I haven't used any humility yet! I have the full complement I was born with.

"Humility isn't thinking less of yourself but thinking of yourself less."[4]

Having humility does not mean you should think lowly of yourself. It means giving yourself and others realistic credit for everything you and they have achieved. But also, it recognizes that most of what you have is a gift. Some people have misplaced pride regarding talents or situations that were given to them and that they did nothing to earn. Good looking, come on, what did you do to deserve that? Tall, did your parents put you on the rack? So, why do you strut around like you are something because of it? In addition, you probably had many life experiences before you were seven years old that prompted you to establish behaviors and preferences. Are you going to brag about your five year old self making these good decisions?

One of your instincts as a human being is to protect yourself. You naturally act in a certain way if you are threatened.[5] Thinking too highly of your talents or situations might create an attachment and/or a false sense of value, e.g. "I have value because I am smart." If you worry about getting your feelings hurt, or what others will think of you, or what will happen if you don't get the thing you really want, your objective thinking may be clouded. Being shy or not speaking up also isn't necessarily being humble either. It could be another form of being overly concerned with yourself. Your lens might be distorted by being either too focused about what others think of you, or by self-loathing.

The faculty to think objectively is reason; the emotional attitude behind reason is that of humility. To be objective, to use one's reason, is possible only if one has achieved an attitude of humility... I must try to see the difference between my picture of a person and his behavior, as it is narcissistically distorted, and the person's reality as it exists regardless of my interests, needs and fears."

—ERICH FROMM, The Art of Loving[6]

Adding the spiritual element, I like St. Thomas Aquinas' definition of humility: "Humility means seeing ourselves as God sees us: knowing every good we have comes from Him as pure gift."[7]

This is not to say you don't appreciate the result of your efforts. It just means you apply perspective. For example, "Thank you God for giving me the desire to succeed or the gift of patience", or "Thank you Lord for giving me the skills and proper environment in which to do well in school."

St. Augustine said in one of his letters, the way to Christ is "first through humility, second through humility, third through humility." He also said, "It was pride that changed angels into devils; it is humility that makes men as angels."[8]

Humility will help to clarify your thinking so that you can more fully entrust yourself to God and His holy will. If you have a strength, accept that as a gift from God. If you have a weakness, accept that as a gift from God. Perhaps you are experiencing a trial on your way to heaven, or the lack of a certain gift has set you on a different path. Rather than complaining about your situation, play the cards that you are dealt.

As noted at the beginning of this section, I struggle with humility. There was a great prayer written by Cardinal Rafael Merry del Val (1865-1930), Cardinal Secretary of State of the Holy See under Pope Pius X. I include this prayer that I say every morning in the appendix, Exhibit I.

In reading this book, be open. Ask questions of other seekers and spiritual guides. Read the Bible and other spiritual books.

Be humble.

Reflection

1. Are you searching to get to know God better?
2. What is standing in your way to go deeper?
3. Evaluate yourself on humility:
4. Go back through those gifts you identified in the last chapter for which you are grateful. How have these free gifts affected your ability to succeed?
5. Do you feel you are better/worse than others? Why?
6. Do you listen to arguments before you form an opinion?
7. Are you fearful about what others think of you?
8. Do you admit when you are wrong?

ON THE FENCE
Stage Three

If God exists and you believe He made heaven and earth, how do you respond to that? Believing in God inspires a nice feeling. It's actually more than just a feeling, because the belief in God is true. It is like a puzzle piece that fits perfectly. And, if you believe in heaven, you want to go there when you die.

If you are here on your journey, you might be wondering why, with all of your understanding of joy, gratitude and humility, you still don't "love God with all your heart, all of your soul, and all of your mind."[1]

Becoming closer to God is not just an intellectual exercise. **Stage three is about going beyond seeking God, to beginning to develop a relationship with God.** How do you start a relationship? Spend time on it. How do you spend time with God? Put yourself in God's presence, i.e. recognize that God is here and available for you.

Love takes time. Love requires investment in the relationship. Loving isn't just a matter of making a decision, for example, "As of this moment, I am going to love you!" It requires multiple decisions to be made that begin with having the right attitude.

You might try to spend time with Him in Mass, through service to others, and through prayer. You can start by adding daily prayer to your life. That person you want to get to know better, you call him up.

Dial-up God! Prayer is the cornerstone of the relationship. Focusing on God throughout the day and making Him part of your life, part of your decision processes, will lift you to new levels of holiness.

Fortunately, God gave us the desire to know him. "Anyone who seeks truth seeks God, whether or not he realizes it."[2]

Search for God and you will find him. Not only is he available to us through prayer, he is in all others as well as all of creation.

Turning toward God is a choice. In fact, personal choices are the only things one can control. At this point you know that getting closer to God is the right choice to make. And you realize you may need to make that choice many times. God instilled in us a desire to know Him. You want to know Him better but you need help. There is one surefire way to grow deeper in your faith—something you can use for the rest of your life: prayer.

"Prayer is the raising of one's mind and heart to God or the requesting of good things from God."[3]

Get off the fence. Pray daily

St. Francis de Sales reputedly said, "Everyone of us needs half an hour of prayer each day, except when we are busy—then we need an hour."

Why do we pray?

Prayer engages you in your relationship with God. Now, God is always in a relationship with us, but often we are not listening or conscious of His presence. Prayer can be joyful, soothing, cathartic, or if we are deep in sin, painful. But like the pain of surgery to remove a cancer, this pain too, will help cure us.

God invites us into a relationship with Him that is both personal and communal. He speaks to us through His Son, Jesus Christ, the Word-made-flesh. Prayer is our response to God who is already speaking or, better yet, revealing Himself to us. Therefore, prayer is not merely an exchange of words, but it engages the whole person in a relationship with God the Father, through the Son, and in the Holy Spirit.[4]

I can honestly say that my morning prayer time is my favorite time of day. Why? Because I sit and reflect on all of the good that God has done for me. I ask for his forgiveness for my sins and I marvel at what he has equipped me with for that day. I almost always finish feeling upbeat and ready for the day.

But why should YOU pray?

Prayer helps orient you. It helps you reflect on God's glory and goodness. In turn, you recognize your dependence on God. You feel better after "counting your blessings". Recognizing that many, if not most of, those blessings came without effort on your part, you cannot help but feel grateful. God is compassionate, forgiving and comforting. What a great way to start the day.

If there is only one thing that you take away from reading this book, let it be to make a commitment to do 15 minutes of morning prayer every day.

Prayer is not just asking for things. God is not a vending machine. You don't ask for something and he gives whatever you ask for. While God always answers, sometimes the answer is "no".

"Prayer is the life of the new heart. It ought to animate us at every moment. But we cannot pray 'at all times' if we do not pray at specific times, consciously willing it."[5]

Types of prayer

The Church describes three types of prayer: vocal, meditative and contemplative. Briefly, vocal prayer is praying out loud. Meditation is a method of thinking about a topic based on what we have read, heard or seen. We react to it and internalize what it means to us. Contemplative prayer is simply thinking about God and our relationship with Him, without props or guides, but just being with Him.[6]

"The need to involve the senses in interior prayer corresponds to a requirement of our human nature. We are body and spirit, and we experience the need to translate our feelings externally. We must pray with our whole being to give all power possible to our supplication.

This need also corresponds to a divine requirement. God seeks worshippers in Spirit and in Truth, and consequently living prayer that rises from the depths of the soul."[7]

"Whether or not our prayer is heard depends not on the number of words, but on the fervor of our souls." [8]

"A blind man when in the presence of his prince will preserve a reverential demeanor if told that the king is there, although unable to see him; but practically, what men do not see they easily forget, and so readily lapse into carelessness and irreverence. Just so, my child, we do not see our God, and although faith warns us that He is present, not beholding Him with our mortal eyes, we are too apt to forget Him, and act as though He were afar: for, while knowing perfectly that He is everywhere, if we do not think about it, it is much as though we knew it not. And therefore, before beginning to pray, it is needful always to rouse the soul to a stedfast remembrance and thought of the Presence of God."[9]

Key to a good prayer habit is having a dedicated time, preferably a dedicated quiet place and having the proper disposition.

How to pray?

While the following describes your actions for prayer, a major part of prayer is in listening to God. So after each element of prayer, spend time in silence, listening.

A simple means to start daily prayer is to use ACTS:

Adoration

Contrition or Repentance

Thanksgiving or Gratitude

Supplication or Petition

Adoration is our response to realizing God is the creator of all things and we would not exist without Him. We praise God for His awesomeness. It lauds God for His own sake and gives Him glory, quite beyond what He does, but simply because He is. After several minutes of adoration, be quiet and listen.

Contrition, or Repentance, is sincere remorse for sin, a resolve to avoid sin in the future and a conversion of the heart, interior conversion. Pause after confessing.

Thanksgiving, different from Adoration, is recognizing not only how wonderful God is in all His works but how wonderful God is to you. Gratitude is the awareness that all you have is a gift and the thankfulness for those gifts. Stop. Smile. Open your mind.

Supplication is the petition for God's help. This is the area that most people—wrongly—think of as prayer. Few will admit this but many prayers go like this: "Lord, I know that I didn't study for the test today, but I would really appreciate you helping me because I want to go to medical school." Listen for the answer. It may or may not be forthcoming but you need to be attentive to God.

I find that adoring God and praising Him aligns my thinking and positions me for an effective prayer. It helps me recognize that I am nothing without God, and that He has done these wonderful things for me. This orients me to be humble (ok, more humble) and confess my sinfulness and thank Him for His goodness to me. It also puts in perspective my "needs" and asks of Him.

I struggled when I initially started daily praying. A consecrated sister suggested I journal as a means of expressing myself. That was almost twenty years ago. I have gone from paper to computer. My need for journaling has almost disappeared, but I like to start each morning with the time and date of the prayer and I type these words, or something similar:

"5:13 6/4. Good morning, Lord. Thank you for this day!"

If anything strikes me, or if I want to refer back to it sometime later, I will jot down my thoughts.

Regardless of how you pray, just remember that "we pray only when there is a lifting of the soul to God. A movement of the heart and an act of the will."[10]

The Catholic Catechism refers to The Lord's Prayer as "the summary of the whole gospel".[11] It is a great start to morning prayer, as you can reflect on each aspect of it. Acknowledge that He is God and praise Him for that, that His will will prevail, that you need His daily assistance and forgiveness, and you ask for help in dealing with people and the issues of the day. Finally, you request God's help to stay on the path. The authors of the Catechism thought enough of it to use the last 98 paragraphs of the book to elaborate on its meaning and beauty.

For further reading, there is a great article by C.S. Lewis where he presents his thoughts on "the Efficacy of Prayer."[12]

Reflection

1. Do you have a prayer relationship with God or are you "on the fence"? If the latter, how will you get off of it?
2. For me, starting my daily prayer life was a matter of commitment. I was not consistent until I decided to set aside the first 15 minutes of each day for it. What are your biggest obstacles to prayer?
3. What do you want to do about the areas you feel you could work on?
4. What would you like to have God do for you?
5. Will you commit to praying for 15 minutes every day at the same time?

DEVELOP A LOVE RELATIONSHIP WITH GOD
Stage Four

You are developing a relationship with God. Through prayer, accurate self-reflection and gratitude, you have developed a desire for God. You still have a lot of questions, a lot of unknowns, and therefore, a fair amount of fear. The question is, do you love Him?

You might say, "Yes he made the world, and me, and gave me all of these cool things. So, thanks, I appreciate it." Is that love? Of course not.

Love isn't just thanks. Or worse, God is not just a being we ask things of. Candidly, that is a very selfish "relationship". You are using God.

Some people might say they love God, but really they are afraid of going to hell. That isn't love. That's an insurance policy!

"Great, Tom. Excellent job of telling us what love isn't. How do you love Him?"

Think about your relationship with God as one would about a relationship with a boyfriend or girlfriend. You spend time together, you talk and you do things for the other person. If God was human, would He want to be your friend? By that I mean, do you talk to God? Are you considerate of God in your day-to-day walk with Him? Are you reverent and go to Mass out of gratitude versus obligation? Do you praise Him and thank Him while you are at Mass, or do you complain about the priest and the music, or are you in your head planning your next vacation?

Love requires the building and nurturing of a relationship. You can't love something or someone that you do not know. What do you love? What do you believe in? In other words, what is your concept of God? Does He interact with the world or does He just observe? Is there a heaven? If there is a heaven, what responsibilities do you have to fulfill in order to be accepted into it? How does God interact with you in your daily routine? Is your prayer only about asking God to give you things or to help with problems? What behavior is required of you as a Christian? What behavior do you feel is necessary that is missing in your life? Why is it missing?

Thankfully, the love of God, and from God, is a supernatural love. It draws us in, if we let it. **Stage Four is about developing a love of God.**

What is love? How do we love?

Let's summarize. We see the prize—living in a loving relationship with God, which results in joy. We express gratitude when we stop and contemplate the many blessings we have received. With humility, our gratitude deepens, as we realize we have been less responsible for our blessings than we thought. This acts as a catalyst to the process of being drawn to God through prayer. Being attracted to someone or something is part of our make-up.

Socrates stated that—and it was further developed by Plato—man has a natural attraction to beauty, truth and goodness. Over time, philosophers have called this a transcendental attraction, or what we might say, innate.

"Beauty draws us to truth, truth leads to goodness, and goodness draws the world back into God's beauty. We encounter beauty when we get a glimpse of the world from the perspective of the beatific vision. Only from this perspective can we see the truth, how things truly are in light of the Gospel. When (and only when) we have the truth, we can begin to be good, albeit imperfectly. When we are good, the lost and broken can catch a glimpse of the divine light borne by the kingdom of God and its means of grace. By becoming citizens of this kingdom, they can begin to see things from God's beautiful perspective. Then, people will see the truth and hence goodness will push back against the ugliness in our fallen world."[1]

You are drawn to truth, beauty and goodness. Something appeals to you that gets you to first notice, and then desire. You like that song. You enjoy spending time with that person. You are blown away by that painting. You want more of that experience and you have found "your passion". You like this thing and it gives you pleasure.

This makes sense, right? I used to think that truth, beauty and goodness was just a nice phrase. Now, I love how God instilled a desire for these three qualities in us to help us choose wisely!

As you grow from childhood, you learn skills and facts, and you make choices based on the input you have received. Many of these choices are made by evaluating and choosing the "better" option. You look at something you think is 'cool' and you move toward it. If it holds your interest, you examine it. If you like it a lot, you desire more of it. This concept of attraction drives so many of our choices, whether they are majors in college, friends or even spouses.

We evaluate things through the lens of truth, beauty and goodness. Our faith refers to these as transcendentals, that is, timeless properties of all people.

The Catholic Catechism has this to say on the subject: "The practice of goodness is accompanied by spontaneous spiritual joy and moral beauty. Likewise, truth carries with it the joy and splendor of spiritual beauty. Truth is beautiful in itself. Truth in words, the rational expression of the knowledge of created and uncreated reality, is necessary to man, who is endowed with intellect. But truth can also find other complementary forms of human expression, above all when it is a matter of evoking what is beyond words: the depths of the human heart, the exaltations of the soul, the mystery of God. Even before revealing Himself to man in words of truth, God reveals Himself to him through the universal language of creation, the work of His Word, of His wisdom: the order and harmony of the cosmos—which both the child and the scientist discover—"from the greatness and beauty of created things comes a corresponding perception of their Creator," "for the author of beauty created them.""[2]

God created truth, beauty and goodness as the means through which we can know Him. We experience life and all of its incomprehensible vastness and complexity. We are humbled that God did this for us and we want to thank Him and be in relationship with Him. We feel gratitude and we want more of this.

As you learn about Him you experience His selfless love, you build trust in that He will never let you down and will forgive your every mistake. Therefore, we value truth beauty and goodness and use this lens through which to choose the "better" option in our decision making and our relationships.

For instance, you develop friendships with those who share mutual likes, and develop an understanding and appreciative love for those people. Furthermore, the natural love between a husband and wife is beneficial for not only reproduction but for receiving and giving love. This reciprocal aspect of natural love helps you continue the process of learning more about that person and appreciating different aspects of their character more and more—growing in love. You have an impulse of the soul. But this love is incomplete. A spouse, being a flawed human, can err, sin or lose interest. All which will wound the beloved.

Aquinas asserts that if one who loves is really "willing the good" that he the lover desires, then he is loving himself. In other words, he is selfish. That is not love. Love is selfless.

I think that statement might come as a surprise to some married couples! Why? They seem to have arranged their marriage as a series of "contracts" or quid pro quo trade-offs. They have expectations of the other to fulfill their needs.

Agape, supernatural love, takes natural love a step further. Somewhere along the way you subjugate your own desire for the sake of the other. It is now a decision to love for the good of the other. It is best expressed in both selflessness through thinking of others and their desires, and sacrifice, because putting that person's desires before our own often causes us to go without, or to do something extra.

The goal is for your "faith to furnish you with a supernatural motive to sanctify your affections. It directs these first, toward God... then, towards God's creatures, which it presents to you as reflections of the divine perfections, so much so, that in loving them you love God Himself."[3]

We love others, whether a spouse or a neighbor, with supernatural love when we will their good solely as an outpouring of the love of God and his creatures. It is a love of God not for what He has done for us but for His being perfect. If we loved God for what He has done, we have gratitude and may love because of the benefits we've received, rather than who God is.

The true endpoint is to love God for being, and then to express that in both loving Him and in loving others.

Reflection

1. Do you love God? What does that mean to you?
2. Do you treat God like you would treat a lover? Do you pray regularly? Do you do things for God (by helping others)?
3. Who else do you love? Is it a quid pro quo love or a selfless love?
4. What can you do next to build your relationship with God?*
5. How can you love God and others unselfishly?

*WE'LL DEVELOP answers to these next two questions later in the book, but for now, spend a minute or two thinking about the need to do something to improve the relationship.

A DEEPER DESIRE TO KNOW GOD
Stage Five

When you develop a friendship, you WANT to learn more about that person. You ask about their family, the schools they attended and cities they lived in. Maybe past jobs they had or interesting hobbies. You learn what opinions and experiences that person has had. You also shape some of your views and opinions through the knowledge gained from those interactions.

Developing your love relationship with God is similar. You want to learn about God. A good first step is understanding what we as Catholic Christians believe, and why. The Bible and the Catechism of the Catholic Church are great resources to study in order to understand what we believe. For those who want the Cliff Notes version you can study both the Apostles Creed and the Nicene Creeds. You will find a short description of these in the Appendix, Exhibit III.

Christianity involves beliefs. An interesting point is that there have many times been arguments within the church about, well, about everything. Over the centuries there have been divisions regarding the divinity of Jesus (seems pretty core to our belief, right?): the belief that Jesus is in the Eucharist; the Apostolic succession; the Assumption of Mary; adaptation of the Bible and its interpretation; and life in the modern world.

The outcome of these discussions has been an incredible collection of information, explanations and exhaustive studies that have provided us with a wealth of not just answers but the reasoning behind those answers.

Why is it important to have a clear interpretation of beliefs? Try to get one billion people to agree on anything! And then have them maintain that belief for 2000 years. The resolution to many issues has been decided upon after studying scripture, researching into writings and oral teachings, conducting debates, and praying—by the early fathers, the great saints like Augustine and Thomas Aquinas, Catherine of Siena and Saint John Paul the Great, and countless other theologians, philosophers and faithful men and women.

I have never been very good with rules. I tend to view them as "suggestions". So, it is ironic that I am going to chastise those who play "fast and loose" with the precepts of the Catholic faith. But here goes.

I find it humorous that a Christian will state, with maybe a nanosecond of thought or research, that "I don't believe that." Sometimes, I would like to scream, "Oh, I see, you know more about the "deposit of faith" than the thousands—no, tens of thousands,—of learned people over the millennia who devoted their lives to study that very issue. You must be remarkable."

But, since I now have great maturity(!) and am trying to be a better Catholic, I normally let it go. On a rare occasion, I might see it as a great teaching moment. It is amazing to me how many times I talk to someone who is mad about some "rule" in the Catholic Church. "I want my daughter's Catholic wedding to be at the beach", "The church is old fashioned on its views about sex", and so on. Occasionally, I have said, "Would you like to know why this is the position of the Catholic Church?" Invariably, after I explain the Church's position, they stop their complaining, and say, "Hmm, that makes sense." (Unfortunately, some issues, like abortion, are not so easily resolved.)

The Catholic Church is guided by the Magisterium, a fancy word for the teaching authority within the church. Headed by the Pope and the bishops, it maintains the integrity of what we promulgate as Truth. It combines both Scripture and Tradition with discernment to codify our beliefs. The Catechism of the Catholic Church outlines many of the beliefs of the Catholic Church and is universally available both online and in book form. In the US, for further details you can also get this information from the United States Council of Catholic Bishops website: www.usccb.org.

Let's clear up a common fallacy, that the Catholic Church is controlled by a bunch of "old white men in Rome". While the leadership is largely made up of older priests and religious, they represent all races and most countries in the world. In addition, they are not sitting around making up new rules and interpretations of established beliefs. They are more concerned with preserving the Truth as it has been transmitted over the centuries. Speaking against the precepts of the Catholic Church is called heresy. Not all heresy is worthy of excommunication or rebuke.

You might be saying to yourself you really don't care about any of this. Nonetheless, at some point during your life you may ask the question, "Why do Catholics believe X?" Too often, people don't consult or look up the reason, but instead come up with their own response based on their limited knowledge and understanding. It is this lack of serious study or examination that has people calling certain rubrics of the Catholic Church "dumb", "outdated" or, heaven forbid, "un-evolved"!

Sometimes, when there is a restriction or sacrifice involved, people choose not to feel obliged. Take one obligation: you must go to Mass every Sunday. "I agree with all of the rules of the Catholic Church, but I don't like the homilies of our priest", "I can't understand our priest", "I am too busy", "That's my golf day". So many things are misunderstood. These uninformed or poorly informed Catholics have been given the rules without the reasons. Here is a short answer to a deep subject:

We attend Mass because it's our loving response to the God who has loved us first. We go not to be entertained or even educated but to praise and thank God in community. In the Eucharist we receive the Body, Blood, Soul and Divinity of Jesus Christ. With this reception we receive graces from God (more on grace in Stage Six). And finally, we go to Mass because God commanded that we "keep holy the sabbath day". We obey the third commandment.

The Catholic Church is beautiful in so many aspects of what it proffers. The more I understand, the more I feel that creation and our relationship with God is spectacular. There is a plan and it is mind-blowing.

There are several mysteries of the Catholic Church for which there are no clear cut answers. In addition, you will most likely encounter confusion, doubt and lack of proof as part of your struggle to believe. These personal shortcomings, introduced by Satan or our own sinful nature, happen to most people even after they have come to believe in the Catholic position. At this point in your faith journey, be open to the fact there is a good possibility the Catholic position is the correct one and you simply have yet to come to that understanding or belief.

The key to learning is to study the information available. **This sixth stage is about desiring to study so as to deepen that relationship with God.**

Study: Explore your faith!

You know intellectually what is right and what is wrong, but sometimes, you hold back. You are afraid of missing out on things. You agree with most of the commandments and rules and regulations but struggle with a few, and are even unaware of a few more.

Being Catholic is a process. It is a continual experience of trying to get closer to God, failing and getting back up again. It takes time. You don't decide to be a world class musician by declaring your goal one day and playing at Carnegie Hall the next. In the beginning there are simple tunes, exercises and lessons in reading sheet music. Then there is the introduction of chords. Then you might play with other people. Throughout this time you are trying to be a better player of your instrument. It takes learning, practice, reading, memorization, and understanding... just like being Catholic.

If you are at this stage, you want more. You sense the goodness of God or you want to feel it. Like natural love, you want to know more and spend more time with God. God created you with this desire to know the good. You have a natural longing to be in relationship with God. Sometimes you are not listening. Therefore, you actively try to go deeper into your faith in a variety of ways, including:

- Asking someone who knows more—a priest, mentor or spiritual guide
- Praying more often
- Going on a retreat
- Going to confession
- Reflection and meditation
- Reading the Bible
- Reading stories about the saints or Catholic encyclicals or other documents
- Joining a Christian fellowship, bible study or accountability group
- Volunteering

This laundry list might seem a little overwhelming. It is meant to give you options as to what fits your persona. I find being in relationships with other seekers is both comforting and effective in faith formation. I especially enjoy volunteering in various ministries because my efforts often help others while I benefit by maturing in my faith.

When you learn about your faith, you can better process what it means. With resources like those above, you can know more about God, appreciate His goodness, and grow more in love.

I suggest reading individual books of the Bible or looking up the Church's position on several issues in the Catechism. Reading the Bible from beginning to end is like reading an encyclopedia from front to back. You might start by reading the four Gospels then the commentary included in the footnotes. Many people like the advice in Sirach or Proverbs. Feel free to ask a priest or friend for an explanation of areas that you don't understand. Both the Catechism and the Catholic Bible, as well as the daily readings for the Mass, are available online or in print. A good resource for Catholics in the United States is The United States Catholic Conference of Bishops (USCCB) website: www.usccb.org

The Catechism is a little harder to find online but is available at either The United States Catholic Conference of Bishops website: https://www.usccb.org/sites/default/files/flipbooks/catechism/ or the Vatican's: http://www.vatican.va/archive/ENG0015/_INDEX.HTM

Use the reflection below to consider what you believe, what you struggle with, and what you are going to do next on your faith journey.

Reflection

1. Read one (or both) of the creeds. What do you believe in? Do not worry about your answer, just probe why you feel that way about your answer.

   1. God created the world and man
   2. Jesus Christ was and is God
   3. Jesus came to save man
   4. I believe in the Trinity
   5. Heaven exists
   6. The devil exists and so does hell
   7. God listens to prayers and acts

2. Other central precepts of the Catholic Church are below. What do you think of the following:

   1. The host and wine are true God
   2. Miracles do happen
   3. Living a life dedicated to do God's will is the key to being joyful

3. Take a moment to look at the gifts God has given you. Look at the gifts you believe in above. Does this elicit a desire to go deeper?

Knowing what you believe and what you question is important for not only getting the answers but for being infused with the knowledge and faith that comes from God alone. Do not be discouraged if you have trouble believing all that you have read or heard. You are on a journey. The answers to many of these questions may take decades for you to resolve.

CHURCH-GOING CATHOLIC... MOSTLY
Stage Six

Who wants to go to Mass? Actually, many people like going to Mass. They go to praise God, thank God and receive the graces of the Mass and Holy Communion. To them, it is not a burden. To some people, it is a joy. They enjoy the community with other believers. They value the Eucharist. (Please see "Transubstantiation" in Appendix, Exhibit IV.) But mainly they are so grateful and they love God, that they want to be there. They are like the dating example in Stage Three where they just want to hang out with the person they love as they navigate their way to heaven. They are grateful and want to experience God's grace.

Let's look at those of us who go to Mass begrudgingly, those who go except for when they're on vacation or at a football game or they're hungover because they drank too much the night before, and those who go only several times a year, jokingly referred to as the ChrEasters —Christmas and Easter-goers.

As a prelude to the discussion on the value of going to mass, let's review your progression so far into a deeper relationship with God. God exists, you believe that . You are grateful for your many blessings and by developing humility you recognize greater the scope of those blessings. You are drawn to God and you love Him. You want to get closer to Him and so you build a relationship through prayer . You love God and want to deepen your faith, so you study it . The Mass is both a personal experience of receiving Christ and also a chance to worship in community.

I believe everyone in this church-going stage wants to go to heaven, but sometimes it just seems like hard work. There are too many impediments to joy. While studying might bring about knowledge and appreciation, you might not feel joyful. Excluding major issues like death, serious illness and unemployment, daily life alone—raising a family, paying bills and unplanned expenses and activities, going to work—can be tough enough for most of us.

There are too many things that compete with going to church. It can seem to be another obligation. At some point, as a Christian, you start going to church. You are either dragged to church as a child, you go because a friend or spouse asked you, or you come to the conclusion you want to try or go back to it. This can result in a warm feeling of self-satisfaction that now you won't go to hell (wrong assumption by the way) or of doing the right thing, like eating one's vegetables. So, how can you go deeper?

If you are not "fulfilled" by Mass, it is up to you to change your perspective. Like a kid who is bored at Disneyworld, there isn't much someone else can do to interest you. You might not always like Mass, but if you go, you will receive graces. And besides, where else will your hear your spouse admit to being wrong :

"I confess to almighty God and to you, my brothers and sisters, that I have greatly sinned in my thoughts and in my words, in what I have done and in what I have failed to do, through my fault, through my fault, through my most grievous fault; therefore I ask blessed Mary ever-Virgin, all the Angels and Saints, and you, my brothers and sisters, to pray for me to the Lord our God."

I don't know about you, but that right there makes it almost worth it!

That said, if you don't like it, it might be hard for you to continue going. You might use your great rationalizing skills to determine that since you are "not getting fulfilled", you don't need to go.

The last excuse is so funny. Let's compare it to two other situations to see the ridiculousness of that statement.

You are dating this fun person and they invite you to a quilt-making class. Your first reaction is, "this sounds dreadful", but you realize you'll be going with your beloved, so you go joyfully. You conclude that the pleasure is in the relationship and not necessarily in what you are doing.

Therefore, if you are not being fulfilled, you might not be putting the right attitude into the relationship. You might need to change your attitude.

Say you want to be a successful athlete. You decide you don't like practice—it's not fulfilling. So you quit. What happens to the goal? It goes unfulfilled. Meeting goals takes work. Being good at anything takes a sustained effort.

In this discussion, you want to get to heaven but instead of working toward that, you don't want to put forth any effort. Is it realistic to expect you will go to heaven based on that choice? Do you think going to heaven is a simple case of checking-off the boxes versus a conversion of the heart? Spoiler alert: The Gospel is replete with Jesus pleading, instructing or chastising the Pharisees to convert.

But how do we change? God wants us to have joy. He certainly doesn't want our relationship with Him to be drudgery. The beauty is, no matter who you are and what you feel right now, God will help you turn the Mass into a joy.

Enjoying the Mass starts with recognizing why you are there. Do you approach it as a means of worship or of obligation? If the answer is obligation, you need grace to help you get into the right frame of mind. See, the Mass is incredible!

The Mass is a joy for many. The Mass provides an opportunity to praise God, thank God and receive the body and blood of Christ, thus earning graces. The whole event is both miraculous and affirming.

You start by remembering you are in the "holy presence of God". You confess your sins and beg for forgiveness. You state every Sunday what you believe in. You are joined with fellow believers who, despite all of their struggles and flaws, show up. What a booster shot for your faith!

"The entire object of true education is to make people not merely do the right things, but enjoy the right things: not merely industrious, but to love industry; not merely learned, but to love knowledge; not merely pure, but to love purity; not merely just, but to hunger and thirst after justice."[1]

If you are at this stage, congratulations for your efforts. But it is not just about having willpower. **Stage Six is learning to obtain grace and use the tools of the theological virtues.**

You need grace.

Grace and the Theological Virtues

"Grace is favor, the free and undeserved help that God gives us to respond to his call to become children of God, adoptive sons, partakers of the divine nature and of eternal life."[2]

The help that God gives us on our journey, grace, is available to all. There are two types of grace: Sanctifying Grace and Actual Grace.

"Sanctifying Grace comes to us when we receive the Sacrament of Baptism. It confers new life in our soul. Sanctifying Grace makes us holy and pleasing to God; it makes us adopted children of God; with it comes the presence of the Holy Spirit to live inside of us. Sanctifying Grace actually gives us the right to go to heaven. Sadly, we can lose Sanctifying Grace through sin. In short, we can lose Sanctifying Grace the same way we can lose our health: by not doing what is necessary to maintain and to preserve it.

Actual Grace is a supernatural help of God which enlightens our mind and strengthens our will to do good and to avoid evil.

Actual Grace comes to us through receiving the other five Sacraments of the Church, and it is also obtained by the prayers we say, the good works we do, and the penances we perform. Actual Grace is only given to us when we need it, to perform a good act, or to overcome a temptation."[3]

There is some confusion by those who say we can merit grace. Jesus participates with us in the reception of grace. It is He that merits the grace for us, not us. Again, it is freely given.

Grace is always available when you need it. You have to be oriented to receiving it. You do that by living your life through the theological virtues.

The Theological Virtues

"Whatever is true, whatever is honorable, whatever is just, whatever is pure, whatever is lovely, whatever is gracious, if there is any excellence, if there is anything worthy of praise, think about these things."[4]

That above quote is a great ideal, but how do you get there? Well, God is so awesome that He gave us tools we can use to be better people so we can get closer to Him.

"A virtue is an habitual and firm disposition to do the good. It allows the person not only to perform good acts, but to give the best of himself. the virtuous person tends toward the good with all his sensory and spiritual powers; he pursues the good and chooses it in concrete actions."[5]

The theological virtues are the cornerstone virtues designed to help us to get closer to God. The theological virtues are directly infused/gifted to us in baptism by God especially for developing our relationship with Him. Unlike other virtues or good habits, which are founded in the theological virtues, the theological virtues cannot be obtained by human effort. In our efforts to exercise them and respond to these gifts, however, God is able to make them grow. Praying for an increase in our theological virtues is important for this reason.

Faith

Faith can be described as belief. I believe in something that I don't know for sure. Faith from a religious perspective is strong belief in God or in the doctrines of a religion, in which there may not be tangible proof of existence.

Faith is the cornerstone of our, ah, faith. We believe in God. We believe in heaven. We believe in Jesus Christ and that through Him we can get to heaven.

God didn't wire us to have to believe in Him. If He did that, it would be certainty, not faith. Why did He do that? Why did He make Himself so elusive? Well, one can argue, are you kidding me? He practically rubbed our face in the Truth!

There are thousands, no, tens of thousands of examples where God came right out and showed us, but we chose not to believe. He created us, showed us beauty and goodness, and even provided us with the ability to bring new life into the world. Did we praise Him in great awe? No, in fact, just the opposite, we have laws that "protect' the right to terminate the miracle of life. God sent prophets and Jesus. Both then and now, we did chose not to believe. We turned from God.

So, how do you build faith? You build a relationship through prayer. As mentioned in the last stage, you spend time studying it. You can read scripture, books on the saints, precepts of the faith or even the Catholic Catechism. You can participate in bible studies, or even encounter groups. On top of those means, God gave us prayer, and supernatural graces.

We read stories in the Old Testament like after God led the Israelites out of Egypt, they built a golden calf to Baal. We say to ourselves, how could they do that? They lacked faith. Even after being rescued, and the parting of the Red Sea! Rather than judge them, look at the absurdity not only in the world, but in each of our lives. "First take the plank out of your own eye."[6]

God gave us free will so we could have great joy. He gave us the ability to choose, fully embrace and appreciate a fraction of His goodness. We in turn, choose to be good.

Hope

"Hope is the theological virtue by which we desire the kingdom of heaven and eternal life as our happiness, placing our trust in Christ's promises and relying not on our own strength, but on the help of the grace of the Holy Spirit.

The virtue of hope responds to the aspiration to happiness which God has placed in the heart of every man; it takes up the hopes that inspire men's activities and purifies them so as to order them to the kingdom of heaven; it keeps man from discouragement; it sustains him during times of abandonment; it opens up his heart in expectation of eternal beatitude. Buoyed up by hope, he is preserved from selfishness and led to the happiness that flows from charity.

Hope is expressed and nourished in prayer, especially in the Our Father, the summary of everything that hope leads us to desire."[7]

Another word for spiritual hope is trust. I trust that God wants what is best for me. Faith is like a petri dish, if you will, that allows one to build hope. "I believe that this is the case. Therefore I trust that these other things will happen."

Trusting in God, letting God be in control, brings graces.

Charity

Emanating from Faith and Hope is Charity. Charity is Faith and Hope in action.

"The Catholic theological virtue of "love" is actually called charity because it has a more nuanced meaning in the Scriptures than does love. It defines charity as means participating in tangible acts of loving-kindness toward all others (friend or enemy) in unconditional and self-sacrificial ways." [8]

Love is the fulfillment of all our works. That is the goal. That is why we run—we run toward it, and once we reach it, in it we shall find rest.

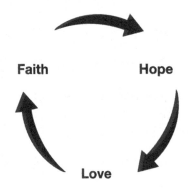

Faith   **Hope**

Love

So, Faith is belief, Hope is a desire for a future good, and Charity is good in action. Incorporating these virtues builds a cycle of belief-desire-action that results in the fruits of charity—joy, peace and mercy—which in turn animates faith. As this cycle of love grows, we participate in church, in service to others and to ourselves, more fully and joyfully.

The success in developing these virtues brings one closer to God. It is the cornerstone to a joyful life of relationship with God.

In my own practice, I find that sometimes I am deficient in one or more of these virtues, and that impedes my ability to progress. I often find I can't improve my weakness by putting more effort into trying to improve that weakness, but I can when I focus my attention on one of the other two areas. For instance, if I am deficient in loving others, I might try to do more frequent acts of faith. This in turn helps me trust in God because my zeal is so strong. The end result is that I have an intense love emanating from this process.

"For by grace you have been saved through faith, and this is not from you; it is the gift of God; it is not from works, so no one may boast."[9]

Reflection

1. What do you get out of church? Why do you go?
2. What can you do to make church-going more enjoyable? I remind myself that I am there to praise God and receive the eucharist and the resulting graces that follow.
3. What will you do next to further develop your "faith, hope and love" with God?

BEING A SUNDAY CATHOLIC
Stage Seven

For decades, our family would go to Mass every Sunday. We had all four of our children receive all of the sacraments. They even went to Catholic school. In my thirties I started a men's fellowship at my parish. After all those years and participation, I have come to realize I had God compartmentalized. Oh, I thought about God and I prayed, but I excluded him from many aspects of my life.

During the men's fellowship, we had members of the group rotate in giving their testimony. One day, the speaker talked about how he had told his friends he went to this church fellowship. He said they thought he was joking, and his realization they were serious really bothered him. He proceeded to tell us about "Good Bill" and "Bad Bill".

Good Bill, he said, went to Mass every Sunday. He prayed, went to confession and generally tried to be a holy person. Bad Bill sinned. Bad Bill occasionally drank to excess, gossiped about others and made lewd comments. Bad Bill might have told a lie to make a sale in business. Bad Bill looked for personal enjoyment, sometimes at the expense of his family. How could this person be a good Catholic and do these things?

There are two main reasons. One, he didn't know some of these things were sins. For instance, I have talked to many people who honestly

believed it was alright to lie in business. I have been told by a lawyer
that he would have to quit his job if he didn't lie. A salesman stated he
needed to create a sense of urgency for the prospective customer. Even
administrators said they did certain things for the good of the
company. Incredulously, they ask, "but that's not wrong is it?" I've also
heard many non-business-related, seemingly innocuous examples, that
demonstrate many people are not aware such thoughts or acts are
sinful.

The more insidious condition is the second one: convincing yourself
your behavior is appropriate. My favorite quote of all is, "Man is not a
rational animal but a rationalizing one." Bill might justify his behavior
by saying he is "letting off steam", or that "flirting isn't cheating", or
he is "providing for my family" or "having some me time". But the
reality is, something else is challenging his sense of right and wrong.

We have desires that are healthy and desires that are inordinate. Just
like each person has different talents and attributes (for example, they
may be six feet tall, highly intelligent or able to curve a soccer ball "like
Beckham") they also tend to have a primary core sin. Many of our sins
rest in three areas: pride, vanity and sensual desire (desire of the
senses, not just sexual desire).

Stage Seven is about trying to be Catholic 100% of the time. To move
past being the Sunday Catholic you can start by doing two things:

1. identify areas where you exhibit certain inappropriate thoughts or
behaviors and strive to eliminate them. You try to be Catholic all of the
time. Once you understand these proclivities, you can establish a
change in behavior as well as some defenses to prevent other behaviors from arising again.

2. You avoid the "near occasion" of sin—you don't put yourself in situations that might lead to sin. When an inappropriate thought enters
your mind, you resolve to dispatch it immediately. You also establish
positive replacements for the sinful thoughts or activities. The challenge might be overwhelming, therefore these thoughts and behaviors
are grouped by core sin to give you an idea where you might concen-
trate your efforts to feel the most impact.

The three core sins[1]

All of us, simply because of our fallen human nature, have sinful tendencies. Saying that we have a "root sin" simply means that for each of us, one of the three sin types is dominant. It's bigger than the others and exerts greater influence on our day-to-day behavior. The three possible root sins are: pride, vanity, and sensuality.

Pride, in this sense, refers to a distorted attachment to our own excellence. The proud person tends to seek meaning and fulfillment in their own achievements and conquests. Vanity is a distorted attachment to the approval of other people. The vain person tends to seek meaning and fulfillment in being appreciated or liked by other people. Sensuality is a distorted attachment to comfort, ease, and pleasure. The sensual person tends to seek meaning and fulfillment in taking it easy and simply enjoying life. Notice that each of these root sins is a distorted attachment to something. The things in themselves—achievements, relationships, pleasures—are not evil. The problem comes when we seek meaning and fulfillment in those temporal, created realities. In fact, we are created and called to seek our meaning and fulfillment in God alone, in our ever-deepening relationship with him. Achievements, relationships, and pleasures are meant to be ordered around and towards that principle and foundation of our life. As the Catechism puts it in #27:

 The desire for God is written in the human heart, because man is created by God and for God; and God never ceases to draw man to himself. Only in God will he find the truth and happiness he never stops searching for."

AGAIN, it is important to realize we each have tendencies that spring from pride, vanity, and sensuality. None of us is exempt from any of them, because we have all inherited a fallen human nature. But in each of us, one of the three sin types is usually dominant. If we can identify which one, we can better aim our efforts to grow spiritually; we can strive to develop the virtues that counteract the cause—the root—of our falls and faults. We can identify this root sin, also called the "dominant defect", by looking at the common manifestations of each. The manifestations which are strongest in your life can help you identify your root sin.

Below you will find a list of these common manifestations. Read through them once, quickly, and make a note of those that characterize you most. You will find that sometimes you succumb to all of them, but one or two will jump out at you as being particularly common or strong in your life. This, or these are, most likely, your root sins.

Common manifestations of pride

- too high an opinion of myself
- annoyance with those who contradict me
- anger if I don't get my way or I am not taken into account
- easily judgmental; putting others down; gossiping about them
- slow to recognize my own mistakes, or to see when I hurt others; inability to seek and give forgiveness
- rage when others don't thank me for favors I do
- unwillingness to serve; rebellion against what I don't like
- impatience, distance, and brusqueness in my daily contact with others
- thinking, "I am the only one who knows how to do things right?" Unwillingness to let others help
- inflated perception of my own intelligence and understanding; tendency to dismiss what I do not understand or what others see differently
- not feeling a need for God, even though I do say prayers
- nursing grudges, even in small matters
- never taking orders
- inflexible in preferences
- always putting myself and my things first; indifference towards others and their needs; never putting myself out for others
- centering everything (conversation, choices,) on myself and my likes

- calculating in my relations with God and with others

Common manifestations of vanity

- always seeking admiration and praise, worrying about not receiving it
- excessive concern about physical appearance
- being guided by the opinions of others rather than principle (this is sometimes called "human respect")
- some types of shyness
- sacrificing principles in order to fit in
- placing too great a premium on popularity and acceptance
- easily discouraged by my failures
- taking pleasure in listening to gossip and hearing about others' failures
- always wanting to be the center of attention, at times stretching the truth, or lying outright, or being uncharitable in my words in order to achieve this

Common manifestations of sensuality

- laziness
- always the most comfortable path—one that requires the least effort
- not going the extra mile for others
- procrastination, rushing at the last minute to do everything
- shoddiness, quick to complain, excessively affected by minor discomforts
- inability to sacrifice
- not doing my part at home
- expecting everyone else always to serve me
- behavior and decisions ruled by my feelings and moods instead of my principles
- excessive daydreaming with myself at the center
- inability to control my thoughts, even if they are not good

- preference for doing only what I enjoy (choice of food, work, and so on)
- uncontrolled and overpowering curiosity; wanting to see and experience everything and every pleasure
- my senses and impulses overrule what I know is right and wrong
- acting out my feelings (frustrations, desires,) with no regard for my conscience, God or others
- only working with those I like; tendency to be easily hurt
- fickleness and inconstancy
- can never finish what I start

For some people reviewing these weaknesses, their core sin will jump out. Others may find they have a mixture of each. It might be difficult to discern which one is the core sin. While you can choose two root sins, it will be very challenging to work on both. Kinda like, "I am going to change all of the things wrong with me, starting now."

It is ok to start with one area and over time realize you have a different root sin. Choose one area and identify the means through which it expresses itself in you. Either write these weaknesses down or make a mental note of them.

When you pray, or relax sometime during the day, evaluate how you are doing. It can be discouraging if you shoot for perfection immediately. What I try to do is look for improvement week-to-week or month-to-month or even year-to-year! I also get much solace when a situation presents itself and I catch myself not committing the core sin. e.g. talking about someone else. Make sure you use these successes to encourage yourself.

Reflection

1. Looking at the examples above, what is your core sin?
2. How does it manifest itself in your life?
3. How will you conquer those thoughts and behaviors?
4. What behaviors do you exhibit outside of church that you want to change?

I WANT TO BE A BETTER PERSON,
A BETTER CATHOLIC
Stage Eight

This knowledge and understanding of grace and the theological virtues is a response to God's call and drives you to a deeper sense of self. You recognize the need to change, to adapt to the self-image you perceive is best. In other words, you strive for a more robust interior life. **Stage Eight is about working on developing a strong interior life.**

Most of life is outside of our control. We are all dealt a hand. Yet, it is often the frustrating or difficult, sometimes even tragic, circumstances of life that force us to face this truth because we are working so hard to keep things under control. When and how have the circumstances of your life highlighted the reality of your vulnerability in the face of so many things beyond your control, like others negative behaviors, the weather, the political state of the country, your upbringing, your child's health?

So what is going on? Through your decisions and the vagaries of day-to-day living, life happens. And if the outcome isn't what you want, then what? In a football, baseball, basketball or hockey tournament, all but one team leaves disappointed with the outcome. Is life not fair for all of those fans of the teams that lost? Many, many things don't go your way. You don't get a good grade in a class. You lose your cell phone. Someone runs into your car. You wake up with a headache. The other person gets the sale. You say something stupid which results in the loss of a friendship. Your love interest doesn't like you back.

It is your life purpose to use the gifts you were given for the glory of God. Do you complain that you didn't receive more? Why? What good will that do? Conversely, do you appreciate the positive impact of the many gifts that you have freely received? Do you realize that many people would love to have some of your blessings?

Even perceived weaknesses might have made you a better or more skilled person. For example, not being athletic might have allowed you to focus on the piano to become a virtuoso! This self-awareness is the beginning of personal and spiritual growth. As you traverse life, you make choices. It's a blessing to have choices. Yet, when choices are made it eliminates other options. When you choose to marry one person, you eliminate all others. The false narrative spread today that choosing marriage restricts freedom is causing people, especially younger generations, to postpone marriage and other commitments. But the reality is, postponing is a choice and the older one gets, the fewer options one has.

Choices have consequences. You can accept those consequences or try to fight them. Fighting them often provoke feelings of "it's not my fault", "it's not fair", and so on, as if life is a board game (well, ok, forget about that game). Since the rules of the game were devised by you, you often end up "winning", for example, you may feel that "these people are mean to me", instead of realizing you were curt towards and dismissive of them. Nonetheless, you realize that this self-orientation, this need to control things or prevent unhappiness, doesn't satisfy.

Some people react to the sports tournament situation by saying, "well, at least it was a good game" while others are inconsolable. Why is the outcome so important to the latter group? Do they "deserve" a victory? Is the coach an idiot for losing? Conversely, do you feel good because your team won, as though you had some role in the contest? Isn't that funny?

The above issues are minor compared to people losing jobs, relationships ending, sickness happening, and lives changing in ways you don't want.

So, if you measure your happiness by desires and expectations, you will many times be disappointed. That does not seem like a recipe for a joyful existence.

I used to say to my children, "Life is not what happens to you, it is how you react to what happens to you."

> *When something happens to you, the only thing you can control is your attitude towards it; you can either accept it or resent it.*

All of this is a long way of saying that the Interior Life is an ongoing recalibration from self-focus, to focus on God and others. Where do you begin an interior life? A great place to start is to have a formal prayer time each morning (or, when you wake up—see Stage Three). Like any relationship, it is critical for you and your friend to communicate. The next step is to accept yourself. How can you internalize what you read or hear if your interior life is cluttered with self-doubt, confusion and unhappiness? Don't worry, that too is a process. Learning to accept oneself is a life long journey. We will never completely get there until we fully trust in God, have hope in the future and radiate His love. But we need to start!

Do some self-analysis. Review your gifts you identified in your reflection on Gratitude (Stage Two). Evaluate yourself using the core sins information in the previous stage. Be open. Be honest. Have faith that God has a plan for you. Trust that He wants what is best. This is not a time for self-flogging, but awareness and gratitude for God's faithfulness. This interactive process will help you deepen your relationship with God.

The Interior Life. Loving and accepting ourselves

We gain possession of our interior freedom in exact proportion to our growth in faith, hope and love."[1]

As stated at the beginning of this chapter, the desire to go deeper into our faith causes us to reevaluate ourselves and our motivations. We search for love and we find that our means of trying to satisfy that love was wrong. In essence, we were loving ourselves selfishly.

"'The kingdom of God is within you,' says the Lord. 'Turn, then, to God with all your heart. Forsake this wretched world and your soul shall find rest. Learn to despise external things, to devote yourself to those that are within, and you will see the kingdom of God come unto you, that kingdom which is peace and joy in the Holy Spirit, gifts not given to the impious. Christ will come to you offering His consolation, if you prepare a fit dwelling for Him in your heart... His communion sweet and full of consolation, His peace is great, and His intimacy wonderful indeed. Therefore, faithful soul, prepare your heart for this Bridegroom that He may come and dwell within you.'"[2]

Those who are at the beginning of the spiritual journey may find the above quote a little over the top. You will find as you grow closer to God, your relationship with Him does become like this, similar to a romantic relationship with another person.

And so, the first step in the interior life is to love oneself. This is not a selfish love but an acceptance of yourself as you are and knowing that you are loved by God. Think about it. People want to have value. They look to others to validate themselves and, because others are human, they are often disappointed. In an age of the perfect body, great wealth and exotic experiences, we are constantly bombarded with comparisons. We develop thoughts like, "If I go scuba diving in the Seychelles I will be happy, because none of my friends have done this".

How do we love ourselves as we should?

Appreciating you have value for simply being, because God made you, opens up a world of hope. Not only were you made by God, but you are loved by Him. He wants a relationship with you. He is always there so it is up to you to complete the connection.

For many of us this is a paradigm shift. People often feel "not good enough" to be loved by God. That is Satan trying to get you to quit.

Others have deep wounds or self-loathing that make the idea of a God loving them unconditionally difficult to accept. Regardless of your circumstances, you are able to turn to God for pardon and peace.

"Do not conform to the pattern of this world, but be transformed by the renewing of your mind."[3]

Through prayer, reflection and the graces that God gives you through the sacraments and otherwise, your heart will change. Loving yourself allows you to love others. This means having the humility to recognize we can't change ourselves, only our attitudes and choices.

"The great secret of all spiritual fruitfulness and growth is learning to let God act. 'Apart from me you can do nothing...Accepting ourselves is much more difficult than it might seem. Pride, fear of not being loved, the conviction of how little we are worth, are all too deeply rooted in us. Only under the gaze of God can we fully and truly accept ourselves."[4]

But this is the great thing. God loves us unconditionally, no matter what. He accepts all of our faults and foibles. He just wants us to return to Him when we sin and ask for forgiveness. Judas betrayed Jesus and could not ask God for forgiveness. Peter denied Jesus and repented. He denied that he even knew Jesus and he is one of the greatest of saints! Their outcomes were not defined by their initial decisions but by their final choices. (Thank you Peter for your humanness.)

I have struggled with self-acceptance much of my life. People often say salespeople are egomaniacs. I have learned that many of us are insecure and need some sort of external validation—a plaque on the wall, an attaboy or attagirl, or just recognition that we have value. By accepting that "this is me", that this is how God made me, I have made progress by turning to God for recognition, and not counting on it from others... as much.

"Love is given freely, it is not deserved, and our deficiencies don't prevent God from loving us —just the opposite! Thus, we are freed of the terrible, disappear-inducing sense that we must become "good enough" to be loved."[5]

We don't have to "waste energy pretending to be what we are not. We can quite simply be what we are."[6]

For more information on the Interior life, I strongly recommend the short book, "Interior Freedom" by Fr. Jacques Philippe, which I have quoted extensively here.

Reflection

1. Do you love yourself? Do you accept yourself for all of your strengths and weaknesses?
2. This isn't to say you accept this is how you are always going to be, it just means you don't beat up yourself or blame others or even fate for the way things are. What would like to change about yourself? How will you do this?
3. How is your work to reduce your sins progressing?

THE STRUGGLE BETWEEN HEART, MIND, AND SOUL
Stage Nine

C oncupiscence. I don't like the word concupiscence because I feel that only a few people really understand the definition within the context of spirituality. In day-to-day usage, concupiscence commonly refers to lust and sexual desire. But its usage in religious scriptures, including within Catholicism, is to more commonly describe an inclination to sin.

"By baptism, all sins are forgiven, original sin and all personal sins, as well as all punishment for sins... Yet, certain temporal consequences of sin remain, such as suffering, illness, death and such frailties as weakness of character and so on, as well as the inclination to sin."[1]

Another manifestation of concupiscence is to desire things inordinately. For example, having a desire to achieve success is fine. Having a desire that includes using or damaging people to get ahead is inordinate, or sinful.

You control many desires in your life. You limit your intake of chocolate, alcohol and food in general. You may want a new TV but you won't steal one. You would rather not go to work but you know you will be fired if you don't.

You use reason to balance the desire and what you perceive as the right decision or action. Making healthy decisions requires restraint. Who wants to be restrained? And there's the rub: no one.

Yet, amazingly, you use restraint many times each day. Why? As discussed in the previous stage, you recognize that actions have consequences. And that decisions both positively and negatively affect you. You prevent some of those negatives consequences with positive actions or restraint. You want to be fit so you try to watch what you eat. You want to be financially responsible so you stick to a budget. You might even want to be thought of as a nice person so you try hard not to talk about others or criticize people.

Often, you rationalize trade-offs. Unfortunately, you also rationalize sinning. You may think that lusting after a particular person isn't really sinning because you are not taking action. And sometimes, we justify sinning, because, well, we like it! And what's more, we don't want to give it up.

Saint Augustine had a great quote: "Lord, please make me chaste, but not yet."[2]

You gotta love that guy! I mean, here is one of the greatest known saints, a doctor of the Church, read far and wide, and he is... human. See? We all have great desires. Controlling those desires is something we must work on throughout our lives.

Externally, you want to "clean up your act" by watching your language, by not complaining or criticizing or talking about others. You reflect on this behavior and try to make amends or corrections to it.

Nonetheless, resisting temptation is not your first concern. Your first concern is to avoid, as the sisters I grew up around used to say, "the near occasion of sin." If you have a problem with alcohol, you don't go to a bar. If you have lustful thoughts, don't go to a swimming pool or any place where your desire may be tempted. You don't put yourself into situations where you may be tempted to sin. **Stage Nine is about actively avoiding the near occasion of sin.**

As said before, getting closer to Christ involves choices.

Temptation

 I can resist anything except temptation."

—Oscar Wilde[3]

Here you are, trying to be the best person you can be, and a lustful thought enters your brain. Or, perhaps your friends are watching a sporting event and there will be a long night of drinking. Maybe you received some money and you have the urge to not report it on your taxes. You overhear some juicy gossip about someone and you just ran into a mutual friend. You look at someone else's life or house and are envious. Your child just tracked mud into the house and you want to chew him out. For some of us, that's just a normal afternoon!

There should be bumper stickers that say, "Temptation Happens!" Worse, you will probably have core sins that repeat... and repeat. More than once you may have said, "God, what is the deal? I am trying to be good and I keep sinning the same sins. Give me a break."

Of course, you know the answer. When Paul said, "I was given a thorn in my flesh, a messenger of Satan, to torment me. Three times I pleaded with the Lord to take it away from me," God replied: "My grace is sufficient for you, for My power is perfected in weakness."[4]

Paul tells us God did that, "in order not to be conceited."[5] I agree. Nothing like a little humiliation to humble oneself.

But I think it is more than that. If God fixed all of your problems, would you have free will? Every option would lead to joy. You would not be perfecting yourself for heaven. (While you can't earn heaven, you are encouraged to "be perfect".)

Resisting temptation not only helps you to not sin, it builds virtues, most notably the cardinal virtues of prudence, justice, fortitude and temperance, as well as the virtue of obedience.

St. Thomas Aquinas describes obedience as something which "unites us to God more than any other virtue, inasmuch as obedience detaches us from our own will, which is the main obstacle in union with God."[6]

The best example of this was Jesus: "Son though he was, he learned obedience from what he suffered; and when he was made perfect, he became the source of eternal salvation for all who obey him."[7]

There are three conditions for something to become a sin: Temptation, Enjoyment, Decision

Prevention

Well the easiest way to not be tempted is to avoid the "near occasion" of sin. I finally found out what this phrase from the old Baltimore Catechism means. Stay away from things that tempt you. Avoid being in a position where you even have to decide to sin or not to sin. It might not be healthy for you to go to a bar with a friend, because you might be tempted to flirt. Flirting might lead to sinful thoughts or worse. Decline invitations to events where there may be a lot of drinking if you think you'll struggle to remain sober. Remind yourself that so and so is a good friend, and prepare your mind to not judge that person when you meet them that day.

Enjoyment

1. Rejection—Displeasure

If something pops into your mind, that is not a sin. That is being human. In order for it to remain not sinful, you must dispatch the thought immediately and not dwell on it. It is best when you have conditioned yourself to outright reject a temptation. Think back to when you were single, perhaps you enjoyed flirting and sometimes took it too far. You are now married and when an opportunity to flirt pops into your head, you do not "go there", instead you declare internally that you are a happily married person. You have conditioned yourself to value your marriage and you see displeasure in breaking your vow. There is no pleasure in the temptation.

2. Denial—Self sacrifice

Sometimes, we may have stopped a particular sin, but we have not lost the desire for it. While desiring the sin is not a sin itself, regretting the fact you can't sin can lead to consideration of sinning and that is dangerous.

Being steadfast in self-denial will lead to future victories and rewards.

Whatever temptations, then, assault you, and whatever attraction ensues, so long as you will refuses consent to either, be not afraid, God is not displeased."[8]

THIS IS where the virtues and the habit of perseverance really prove their worth. Resisting temptation is a lifelong condition and the more one is prepared for it, the better. While you may never master the state of displeasure when tempted, you must commit to never consenting.

Since this state is easier to reject than the next, it is best to take some time to reassure yourself why this rejection is important and offer up the struggle to God.

Consent

We either walk away or we consent to the temptation. This could be an impulse and we jump in, or it could be a slow internal debate, or a non-decision—for example, not removing oneself from the temptation —that puts our situation in peril, and we succumb. You might success-fully not gossip about someone with a mutual friend, but then that friend says something negative about that person. Instead of changing the subject immediately, you pause and your friend goes on. At which point, you recognize it is wrong and you just blurt out some gossip. You feel bad afterwards but something inside you made you want to say something so that you came off as fun, smart or cool.

Unfortunately, we all sin. As we discussed in the section about core sins, we sin repeatedly. The devil does some of his best work in these cases. He makes you feel bad about yourself. He gets you to quit, lose hope or rationalize while it is okay to commit the sin. We may think things like "I have made so much progress—now and then a little sin won't hurt me." Or, "If I need to do this one sin in order to be a good person overall, so be it. It is what I need to do."

Perseverance

So, the most important thing to remember when we sin is to not give up. It is important to feel contrition, ask for forgiveness and then try not to sin again.

"Our Lord fell on the way to Calvary. That is significant. If the cross becomes so heavy for us, His disciples, that we let it fall along the road, do we take it up again to follow the path to the heights that it beckons us on? Or do we give way to discouragement?"[9]

Why do we persevere? Why do we continue to carry our cross? The devil and the world offer us false hope. We must choose, daily, to resist. This resistance might seem very hard, even futile, but you will be equipped with good habits to succeed. If you fail, be contrite, go to confession and vow to get better. Just like you might sneak a dessert or eat between meals while on a diet, you have to recommit to reach your objectives. Quitting is the only sure way to fail. Perseverance with a life of prayer and commitment to be good will lead you to holiness. The reward is great. In fact, it is heavenly.

Reflection

1. With your core sin front of mind, where do you see your greatest temptations?
2. What practices can you adopt to ensure you avoid the near occasion of sin in these instances?
3. What methods can you use to stop the thought or circumstance when it occurs?
4. What means can you employ to resist consenting to the thought?
5. How will you handle the results of your sinning?

COMMITTED CATHOLIC
Stage Ten

As a committed Catholic you want to go deeper in your faith. You are now at a place where you seriously want to eliminate sin from your life. You see the value in restraint, being good and that heaven is for real.

You recognize the need and even have some desire to go to Mass every Sunday, even on vacation. You go to confession at least once a year. You belong to a Fellowship or prayer group. Most likely, if you are one of these Catholics, you don't reject any Catholic teaching but you believe your lack of understanding or lack of faith is why you are uncomfortable with certain beliefs.

HOW do you go deeper into your relationship with God? Going deeper means changing. Some changes may be refinements and some might cause you to say, "holy cow. I don't know if I can do this."

Pope John Paul II wrote an apostolic letter entitled, Novo Millennio Ineunte (At the close of the Great Jubilee of 2000) to the Bishops Clergy and Lay Faithful. Many theologians and religious followers were expecting him to announce his retirement from active ministry. Instead, the letter begins with:

"At the beginning of the new millennium, and at the close of the Great Jubilee during which we celebrated the two thousandth anniversary of the birth of Jesus and a new stage of the Church's journey begins, our hearts ring out with the words of Jesus when one day, after speaking to the crowds from Simon's boat, he invited the Apostle to "put out into the deep" for a catch: "Duc in altum" (Lk 5:4). Peter and his first companions trusted Christ's words, and cast the nets. "When they had done this, they caught a great number of fish" (Lk 5:6).

Duc in altum! These words ring out for us today, and they invite us to remember the past with gratitude, to live the present with enthusiasm and to look forward to the future with confidence..."[1]

Pope St. John Paul was calling for us to join him in going deeper. If an eighty-one-year-old man can make a commitment to go deeper in his faith, I guess we can too. He knew this effort would not only bring us closer to Christ but also empower the "New Evangelization".

You too, want to go deeper. You have seen either in your mind's eye or through the examples of other people the joy that can come from Christ, and you want that.

To go deeper, you need God's grace. Prayer, the Eucharist and confession all contribute to being in a place from which you can accept change.

That said, you may not want to change. You may be comfortable in the state you are in, fearful of missing out, anticipating loss as a result of this restraint, or you may not to feel controlled. I get that. We all want to keep our options open. As I have mentioned before, many people go through life without evaluating themselves and taking action. But we should realize that not making a decision is a decision, and it has consequences. For example, being dissatisfied with your present job but not looking for a new one is making a decision to stay in your current job, at least until you make another decision. Stage Ten and the next two stages are about finding more means of going deeper into your faith, as opposed to being stages in themselves. Nonetheless, I incorporate them as stages as they are commonly used means for progression. **Stage Ten is about a more frequent self-review of thoughts and behaviors**. It is exemplified by you performing a nightly examination of conscience.

Jesus calls us to conversion: "The time is fulfilled, the kingdom of God is at hand; repent and believe in the gospel."[2]

The examination of conscience

There is a maxim: that "in order for something to improve, you have to measure it." In other words, if you don't reflect on how you are performing with a particular activity, you have no data to confirm if you are getting better or worse at the activity.

The Apostle Paul wrote in his first letter to the Corinthians that an examination should be performed by the faithful each time they received Holy Communion: "But let a man examine himself, and so let him eat of that bread, and drink of that cup. For he that eateth and drinketh unworthily, eateth and drinketh damnation to himself... For if we would judge ourselves, we should not be judged."[3] This was later prescribed by the Church as a means for sanctification, an examination of conscience.

When most Catholics think of an examination of conscience they think of preparation before confession. A detailed examination of conscience before confession often follows the outline of the Ten Commandments and/or the precepts of the Catholic Church. There are various ways to do this. Some simply review the ten commandments in their head and some refer to a sheet with an expansive list of examples of ten commandments sins. (See Appendix, Exhibit V.)

In addition to this detailed periodic review of sins, a nightly examination is an excellent tool with which to measure progress, to ask God for graces to improve and to allow time to grow closer to God. Who wouldn't want to do it? Well, I didn't, for one. At one point in my prayer life, I was already religiously (pun intended) performing a morning prayer ritual, going to daily Mass, doing spiritual reading and thinking about God often during the day. Why do more? I finally started performing a nightly examination and I found it to be very important as I advanced along the path of spirituality.

Why did I not want to do an examination? Well, I thought that I was doing enough, and I certainly didn't want to beat myself up by reviewing all the bad things I did that day. Yet, if all I did was look at my errors, I probably wouldn't continue doing it. Several advisors have suggested that I also include questions like, "where did I see God act in my life today?" And "what successes in handling my core sins did I exhibit today? This thoughtful review of positive things that happened balances out the reflection on sinful behavior and has made this a wonderful prayer time with God.

The Examen prayer then is an overall reflection on how you felt God's presence in your life that day. In review of the day, you might try to discern what God might have been telling you through the circumstances of your life, and reveal where God is leading you now.

After doing this for several years, I asked Julie if she wanted to pray with me each night. Not only does this ensure we do it, but I have come to appreciate Julie's faithfulness. Plus, I gotta tell you, I love it when she thanks God for me or for some specific action I took that day! It is two-five minutes a night well-spent.

Here is the Examination At Night process that Julie and I use:

- Place yourself in the presence of God, and bless yourself
- Start by praising God for all of His many gifts. This puts you in a good frame of mind (and often a good mood, too!) Silently review the challenges of the day or reflect on the behavior that you are working on in your Program of Life. (See the next Stage) Identify what they might be and what you are going to do about them
- Reflect on what you think God was telling you that day and what you might do with that information. Add to prayer, make a change or simply thank God?
- Recognize that God forgives you and is pleased with your effort
- Recite the Lord's Prayer, the Glory Be, the prayer of St. Michael and the Memorare
- Perform the sign of the cross

Reflection

1. Examine your reluctance to perform an examination of conscience. What challenges keep you from being enthusiastic about it?
2. Identify reasons why making a nightly examination of conscience will help you.
3. Know that God forgives you. Forgive yourself.
4. Start performing a nightly Examen. Make sure to include successes and good experiences of the day. Thank God for those.

CONFORMING THE INSIDE
WITH THE OUTSIDE
Stage Eleven

A t this point you are being referred to as "the Church Lady" or "Mr. Knights of Columbus". You may be volunteering for apostolate works within or outside of your parish as well as assisting with different tasks or committees for the parish. You feel good when you do things for the Church. In fact you don't consider it work because you like those with whom you perform the service.

Unfortunately, you are also most likely noticing the flawed nature of all souls, even those serving the Church. This may be a time of spiritual warfare. You may be thinking, "I am going to change churches because I think the pastor is…", or " I can't believe a woman like that considers herself to be a good Catholic!"

Realize this is often a time of great spiritual fulfillment. More of your activities are performed out of gratitude than obligation. You see the beauty in different elements of the Church and are glad to be a Catholic. Thus, you may like being an Adoration guardian, participating in retreats such as Cursillo, Welcome, and Marriage Encounter, or bible studies likeWalking with Purpose.or Encounter with Christ. You may be going to Mass several times a week because you are grateful and you want to get closer to God.

One challenge at this stage is to not confuse busyness with holiness. We are called to "be" a Christian, not to "do acts" like a Christian. You want to help others come closer to Christ and not be recognized for it. But even when we don't intend to do things for recognition, we sometimes get caught up in the attention and approval. We are conflicted.

Why is this so difficult? Why do we spend so much time thinking about ourselves? First, you need to think about yourself and your situation as part of God's design for your existence. You feel a gurgling in your stomach and you say to yourself, "I am hungry. I am going to get something to eat." Or, you open the door and notice that it is thirty degrees outside, so you think, "I will get a coat."

Thinking about yourself isn't a bad thing to do. It is necessary for survival and personal development. You may be struggling with certain impediments to spiritual growth. Or, you might simply have some questions about how you react to why Catholics do this or believe that. You want to understand these things and grow closer to God. But you feel like you need help.

While trying to sort all of this out, you need feedback on your priorities and the means you are using to effect change. You know your core sins and you are performing a nightly examination of conscience but you see too much repetition of sins and not enough progress. You may feel like you are caught up in "doing" versus "being". **Stage Eleven is about getting external feedback to enable you develop a true understanding of your progress and provide you with suggestions for improvement.** This is often accomplished by having an accountability partner (or group) or a spiritual director.

A popular tool you can use, with or without a coach, is called a program of life.

A program of life is a game plan on how you want to live your life and the changes you need to make to get there. It does not have to be a long document as long as it addresses three areas:

1. A review of your prayer life and other spiritual commitments such as confession and spiritual reading

2. A plan to build virtues or eliminate vices
3. A review of how well you perform in your daily roles, as a spouse, parent, colleague and so on

A great way to build this plan and monitor your progress is to review your plan and performance with either an accountability group or a spiritual director. Can you be a good Catholic without having a spiritual director? Sure. Can you be a good golfer without a coach? Yes. But if you want to be a better golfer, and want to improve more rapidly, get a coach. If you want to get deeper into your faith, have someone guide you in your commitments and hold you accountable. There are often either things you were not aware of, or practices you might do to speed up your spiritual development.

Spiritual direction

This book is dedicated to the spiritual directors I have had in my life. Why? More than anyone else, they have helped me grow deeper in my faith and in my love of God. I am eternally grateful to them.

First, what is spiritual direction?

"Spiritual direction is a 'gathering together' of two in the name of Jesus, the spiritual director and the directee, to help a person to develop a closer relationship with God and to better discern how the Holy Spirit is leading in their life."[1]

"From the point of view of the person receiving it, spiritual direction is an extremely useful (many would say essential) help for growing in holiness, which is the same thing as growing in one's communion with God, which is the same thing as growing in authentic wisdom and happiness. Having a spiritual director is like having a coach: they keep us objective and accountable, warn us of pitfalls, encourage us when we feel weak or discouraged, help clarify confusions and doubts, and make sure we are working intelligently in our efforts to know, love, and follow Jesus Christ more each day."[2]

Spiritual direction can take many forms, based on where you are in your faith journey. You typically meet monthly with your director and either follow a specific framework such as the program of life, or discuss issues in your life. It is not psychoanalysis. It does not necessarily include confession. It is a means of probing the spiritual elements and struggles of ordinary life.

You can ask your parish priest or parish office how to find a spiritual director in your community.

Reflection

1. Do you have anyone who formally holds you accountable? If you don't, are you able to seek an accountability partner or spiritual director?
2. Will you meet with your accountability partner regularly?
3. Do you prepare for and perform any suggestions your partner gives you in your accountability sessions?
4. Sometimes, out of fear of being judged, we hold back. Do you? How can you become more open?

GETTING RID OF THE OLD SELF
Stage Twelve

P raying becomes a more frequent part of your day. Besides morning prayers, you might say the Angelus at noon, night prayers in the evening and perform an examination of conscience. During the day you may think about God and say a short prayer of thanks or ask for help in being faithful.

In your evening reflections, you may realize more and more that your past behavior was sinful or simply disingenuous. For instance, you may have done things for others so they liked you as opposed to doing them selflessly. You may come to see that you did a lot of things with a quid pro quo ("this for that") mentality rather than having a selfless heart. You realize your past self-centeredness.

Or, you may have been very controlling. As part of that, you told people what to do and were very critical. You discern, begrudgingly, that you used control to cover up your insecurity or lack of self-worth.

A different personality might approach interactions in a passive-aggressive manner instead of an outwardly controlling manner. If this is the case for you, you may have realized that your hesitancy to present your view to others is driven by a fear of failure. You might even have rationalized that you are a "nicer person than that" so you didn't get into confrontations, but in reality, you are upset and you plot a horrible death for that person. I mean, you don't think nice thoughts about that person.

In any case, as you become more in touch with your flaws, you learn more about why you do some of the dumb things you do. You also realize that some of the selfish things you did in the past are more insidious than you thought. This is challenging. You feel bad. Fortunately, you are recognizing that God loves you and you forgive yourself, and you vow to keep trying to get better. You are more accepting of others and you stop yourself when you judge. Most of the time, you try to redirect conversation from gossip. You try to have, and to project, a positive image.

This is a period of frequent personal adjustment. This is not driven by insecurity as much as a desire to be the best you can be. You catch yourself before you say that incredible funny, but off-color comment. You hold your tongue when you think about something good you have done and refrain from bringing it into conversation even though there is a perfect place to state it. You want to not just avoid sin but increase in perfection.

All of this requires work, and it sounds exhausting. Yet, God created an amazing being that can take all of this in stride. You are equipped to process and handle many things without consciously thinking about them.

Imagine, for example, you are sitting in your office and across the street is a coffee shop. You decide to get a cup of coffee. You cross the street, you open the door to your office building, look both ways so you don't run into anyone, notice a man with a dog, make a comment to yourself about how tall that woman is, look for cars so you can cross safely, then you make sure you step down from the curb so you don't fall, look both ways again, recognize the car passing is a Ford, decide your next car will be a Mazda, start to walk, remember you are to stop at the store and bring home milk, step up on the curb, check the sidewalk for traffic, notice the hiring sign in the window, and open the door, making sure no one will be hit by the door when you open it! It sounds exhausting but this is what your brain is processing in the background. You learn habits and skills to get you to the point where you are conscience of the important elements while others take care of themselves. Just like self-reflection!

You may or may not have a spiritual director at this time. Whatever your situation, you need some additional tools in your toolkit for personal growth. God just happens to have several at your disposal. **Stage Twelve is about actively utilizing the tools of Prayer, Fasting and Almsgiving.**

Prayer, fasting and almsgiving

How do you become a better person? Through conforming the will and conversion of the heart. Mortification is another word I don't like. It reminds me of someone in the middle ages wearing a hair shirt. Mortification may be defined as "the struggle against our evil inclinations in order to subject them to the will, and the will to God."[1]

"Mortification has a part in the cleansing of past faults, but its chief purpose is to safeguard us against sin in the present and in the future, by weakening in us the love of pleasure, the source of our sins."[2]

"Scripture and the Fathers insist above all on three forms, fasting, prayer, and almsgiving, which express conversion in relation to oneself, to God, and to others."[3]

In fact, Jesus in the Bible doesn't tell us to pray, fast and abstain, He assumes that we do. He tells us how to do each more efficaciously.[4]

Prayer

The cornerstone of an interior life is a strong prayer life. We have talked about prayer often, but in this section I want to focus on Adoration before the Blessed Sacrament.

Adoration can be a period of quietness in study or prayer. For some, it's a structured time of devotion. I prefer to define adoration as "wasting time with God". Like the example of when you are dating someone new. It's exciting, you don't care what you are doing, you simply want to spend time with that person. Yet, I think the highest form of it is simply contemplating God.

"Anyone who has a special devotion to the sacred Eucharist and who tries to repay Christ's infinite love for us with an eager and unselfish love of his own, will experience and fully understand—and this will bring great delight and benefit to his soul—just how precious is a life hidden with Christ in God and just how worthwhile it is to carry on a conversation with Christ, for there is nothing more consoling here on earth, nothing more efficacious for progress along the paths of holiness."[5]

So, again, in praising God, in simply experiencing God, we get outside of ourselves and become more God-oriented. Beneficially, through spending time with Him through adoration, you become joyful.

Fasting

Fasting is a wonderful way to discover how attached you are to something. When you give up something for Lent, it seems like almost every day there is a great opportunity to indulge in the thing you have given up.

We go without (or we do extra) in order to build virtue and to please God. Externally, we do so joyfully, yet internally, there is pain, regret, hunger, and we offer that up as means of penance.

As our first and foremost means of victory over self, we should seize those myriad opportunities that are offered to us to resist temptation, to correspond to the inspirations of grace, and to accept cheerfully whatever suffering comes to us."[6]

WHAT I LOVE SO MUCH about God is that when you try to do something for Him, He has built in so many side benefits for you. As the saying goes, "you cannot outdo Christ's generosity to us". And so, self-denial builds habits and virtues such as temperance, obedience and the ability to put others or something more important ahead of our fleshly desires.

I love and hate fasting from food. (There are many things that you can fast from—television, the internet, a favorite hobby.) I am a foodie. I like to eat, I savor what I eat and I think about the next meal and what I might have, immediately after eating. Fasting from food is hard for me. Yet, it provides so many benefits.

When I get hungry, one of my first thoughts is, "I am doing this as a sacrifice." This results in me actively giving thanks to God. It brings my passion under control. It helps build the virtues of perseverance, temperance and patience: "This too shall pass."

This practice particularly builds fortitude in resisting temptations in future situations.

Going without also helps me appreciate what I have, maybe even recognizing that others don't have what I have given up. The result is increased gratitude for what I have, and thanks to God, and possibly the desire to help others in these areas.

Almsgiving

Almsgiving, or giving away money or goods is a response to God's grace. It is a form of fasting, or going without. It is a way to live out our gratitude by benefiting others. Additionally, it forces you to think of things other than yourself. It causes both sacrifice in the loss of goods as well as joy in seeing the results of giving.

Donating money, time or goods is a wonderful way to redirect your thoughts from yourself. You take the thought process away from you and instead think of helping others. Again, by being obedient, God rewards you with healing.

In each of these three areas, God gives you a tool to get outside of yourself, to help you move away from thoughts such as "what's in it for me?" or even "poor me".

Often in life, things don't go your way, or something you planned on happening, doesn't. An accident occurs. A mistake was made that causes you harm. Or life happens and you suffer. "Why, O lord when I am trying to be so good, do I continue to suffer?" We need to accept it and continue. These tools help us to persevere.

We lack courage because we lack love. What means did Christ choose to redeem the world? He chose sacrifice.[7]

Reflection

1. Do you have a scheduled Holy Hour at your church? Would you consider creating or attending one?
2. Do you fast? In what way do you feel you should fast?
3. Are you often selfless? Do you do things for others and for God out of love for them without looking for something in return?
4. Do you donate money to the point of sacrifice? Do your donations cause you to go without?

EXPERIENCING GOD THROUGH OTHERS
Stage Thirteen

F or most of this book I have suggested going internally within prayer or study to achieve a stronger relationship with God. While this is certainly an effective means, it isn't the only one available. In fact, God utilizes all of nature to draw us closer to Him. **In stage thirteen you will see the active hand of God operating in others.**

I remember being conflicted once about a decision regarding our family. I prayed and prayed, went to adoration, read spiritual books for insight or inspiration and even lit candles! Nothing. One morning Julie walked into the room and said, "I think that we should do…"

Once I recovered from the great wounding to my pride ("Hey, I have been doing all of this praying. Why didn't you tell me?"), it hit me like a ton of bricks. "Oh my gosh, God is answering through Julie!" In fact, without me recognizing it, He has been working through Julie for much of our marriage. Since then, I have often asked Julie for her thoughts on many more issues as a means of determining God's will. Not only does she have good insight, but she is a godly woman, who also prays for understanding. I believe God has used her often for answers to MY challenges.

He has used others also.

Your road to joy starts with the desire to know Him. As mentioned earlier, realizing that God created you purely out of love, that you have value simply because He created you and you exist to experience and share that love, often causes gratitude. But if your focus is just on you and God, you might be missing out.

We may come very close to God through prayer and through reading the Bible or other spiritual books, but we can also experience the joy of God's creation through conversation and just spending time together with others who are working on being better Christians.

A great means of spiritual growth is observing how others model Christ. In seeing others you might ask yourself, why does he or she do that? Why does that bring her joy? And hopefully, where do I go to get me some of that? Interacting with other Christians often leads you to be encouraged, to know that you are not in this alone, let alone that you are not nuts for being countercultural! We all need encouragement. God provides that in prayer, the sacraments, through others and in miracles.

Miracles

Some people have experiences of God interacting with them through words or deeds. We call inexplicable events, outside of natural phenomenon, miracles. Miracles often touch us deeply and facilitate a profound connection with God.

Candidly, I experienced a miracle when my son was in a coma following a horrible car accident. My wife and I prayed one night and I said, "Lord, we have four wonderful children. We offer our son back to you." But because I was a salesman, I then started making a case for why it would be a good idea to heal him!

That night, at around one in the morning, I felt God impress upon me, "I am giving your son back to you." I immediately woke Julie up and told her. When we went to the hospital early the next morning, our son's brain pressure had improved to such an extent the prognosis had changed from almost certain brain damage to no damage. I asked the nurse when it had happened, she said about one or two a.m. The doctor later told us there was no logical reason for the brain's swelling to reduce in one night. This event was like a booster shot to my faith— a catalyst that helped me go deeper. It brought clarity and conviction.

It had a profound impact on me, my family, and those who were around us, and our son at that time. Strangers had prayed for my son and were thrilled with his recovery. Now, some people thought, "I am happy for them but it was just his body healing." That's a funny thing about human nature. You can be adamant about the truth of your own miracle but skeptical when someone tells you about theirs! Think about people's reactions to Jesus' miracles. God wants us to get closer, but only if we choose to. He presents us multiple situations and examples to help us choose Him.

I have come to believe that miracles are not rare. The changing of water and wine into the body and blood of Christ happens millions of times each day. Why do we fight accepting these glorious encounters?

Yes, some things which have been historically considered miraculous have later been explained by science. Yes, when Aunt Clara calls to tell you is a miracle she found her lost glasses, you roll your eyes. And many things are hard to believe. Well, many instances may not be miracles. But, and here is the key, many are. Some people resist believing in miracles out of pride and a need to control their understanding of the world.

It takes reflection, contemplation and/or prayer in order to believe. The key is to use your experiences or the hearing of others' experiences to change your life. Unfortunately, this is not a straight path. You make progress, fall back, and meander. Through this process you need to continually choose Christ.

In my case, it practically took multiple baseball bat smacks to the side of the head to really make the changes that God was calling me to make.

One thing I love about God is that He created man to be in relationship with others. We can look at two lovers interacting or at how parents interact with their children and we see the similarity in how God relates to us. We see and experience love and can model that for how we can love Jesus.

Reflection

1. Do you share your views and feelings about God with others?
2. Can you see God operating through these people?
3. Have you, or has someone you are close to, experienced a miracle?
4. What impact has that had on you?
5. What do you want to do now in your relationship with God?

SPIRITUAL DRYNESS
Stage Fourteen

W hile I hate that Mother Teresa suffered so with spiritual aridity, I like having a relatable example of a true saint who suffered in this way. I once heard that attributing superhuman virtues to a saint is denigrating their efforts to be holy. In other words, perseverance in times of spiritual dryness proves the mettle of many a saint. **Stage Fourteen is about accepting suffering and use it to go deeper.**

"Nothing is more pleasing to God than unshakable faith and confidence in the midst of darkness. Practice acts of confidence even when you feel nothing." [1]

 The deepest wound that is dealt to our soul by sin is that of self-love, by which, in practice, we continually attribute to ourselves the good that we do. To heal us of this wound, Jesus often allows us to prove what we are without Him, that is to say, Nothing!"[2]

WHILE SPIRITUAL DRYNESS is not in a set place on the path to holiness, you will most likely encounter it at some point. It seems you receive more graces as you begin your faith journey than you do later on because in the beginning you need them in order to persevere.

In my case, I noticed I receive far fewer consolations from God now than earlier in my faith journey. When I was starting Southern Catholic College I felt God calling me to do it and I had many reinforcing moments. As I proceeded along the path, the consolations became less and less frequent. Initially, I was wondering if I was doing God's will. When I didn't get any indication one way or another, which was most often the case, I would just say to myself, "Well, ok, this is what makes sense for me to do today." And that is what I would do.

In retrospect, I realized that at the time I had sometimes used God as a vending machine. Here is my prayer token, please drop into the receptacle the solution that I picked. In the faith maturation process, God took me to the next step. He got me to realize it wasn't my effort that made things successful, it was my trust in Him. He began helping me by forcing me to put my trust in Him rather than interpreting signs and having consolations for my decisions.

I liked knowing what was next. I felt good and, yes, a little prideful. It was mentally draining as I scrambled for certainty. Removing the certainty has helped me rely on God.

I think that if you know why you are suffering, it is easier to accept. In preparation for athletic contests, you may be sore, tired and emotionally depleted. You accept it as part of the training. Well, God is preparing us for heaven. We might not understand why we suffer but He brings good out of it for our salvation.

Accepting suffering

Of course we should try to avoid suffering. I am not crazy. We have a God-given talent for avoiding it. For instance, we learn not to put our hand on a hot stove. We look both ways before we cross the street. We study hard to get a good job to be free of poverty.

So what am I talking about? Why accept suffering? It is easy to understand why many of us have doubts and feel confused about God's role in our lives, let alone have belief that He is what fills the emptiness.

War, violence against others, famine and other natural disasters all beg the question, "why?"

First, suffering is a part of life. We are not going to discuss why there are tsunamis, why kids get cancer, or even why God invented Poison Ivy. As mentioned before, this is not heaven. These things are part of our world, part of our existence. Our earthly life is to freely choose God and work on sanctification. If everything was easy there really wouldn't be a choice because all choices would have positive outcomes. Therefore, as we need to accept ourselves, we need to accept suffering. This does not mean enduring suffering that can be removed without sin. You clean and put ointment on a cut. To not do so would be to abuse your body. But suffering that you must endure, you should accept as a grace.

In college, I applied to medical school. I thought that being a doctor would be cool and I would make a good income. When I received my final rejection, I cried. God had a better plan. I chose another path—a new industry called software. I was successful enough to own and sell a business. I tell people that getting into medical school was one of the best things that never happened to me!

"We should accept things as they are. Life is good and beautiful just as it is including the burden of suffering. Yet, man has a thirst for truth, a need to understand, that is part of human dignity and greatness."[3] So, we ask, "why?" Why, when we are trying to be the best we can be, does this happen to us?

In today's world, we expect everything to be fixable. In addition, we measure ourselves against others and covet their goods, successes, looks and situations. It is easy to see how having that orientation can lead to misery. The adage "count your blessings" is sage advice for a happier life.

One of the beautiful things about God's grand plan is He lets you cooperate with Him. You are able to freely choose. At this stage of faith, you are trying to put your trust in Him. You are trying to choose God's plan for you. You should not be resentful and go through the motions but instead, consent to the suffering.

"The need to understand what is happening when we are undergoing a trial is sometimes simply an expression of an inability to abandon oneself trustingly to God and a search for human security. We must be purified of that."[4]

The challenge is not to say, "why do these things happen to me?" but to say "what am I going to do about it?" Again, you might be able to alleviate the suffering, but if not, how will you endure? Will you accept it gracefully? Will you offer it up? This pain may achieve a greater good. Even if the pain doesn't achieve some worldly benefit, you can use it for sanctification. You can offer it up. You can say, "God, your plan is better than my plan. Help me be humble. Help me be thankful!"

"The most important and most fruitful acts of our freedom are not those by which we transform the outside world, as those by which we change our inner attitude in light of the faith that God can bring good out of everything without exception. Here is a never-failing source of unlimited riches. Our lives have in them anything negative, ordinary, or indifferent. Positive things become a reason for gratitude and joy; negative things an opportunity for abandonment, faith, and offering it up."[5]

Reflection

1. Has there been a time in your life where your suffering turned out to be a disguised good?
2. What challenges do you face in accepting suffering?
3. What sacrifices do you offer to God?

BEING OTHERS-ORIENTED
Stage Fifteen

W e have covered a lot of ground. You are now a prayer warrior. You understand the concept of "praying without ceasing" as spontaneous prayer and thoughts of God happen throughout your day. You know that He knows what's best for you. You love God almost as you would love a lover.

As you navigate the path toward holiness, you want to please God. Therefore you become more "others" oriented. Instead of focusing on yourself (pride), what others think of you (vanity), or your various wants and pleasures (sensuality), you move to thinking of God and accomplishing things for His glory. This drives you to consider others. You look at your neighbor and want the good for him or her. You want them to succeed and not fall off track and sin.

I used to be a huge joke teller. Notice that I didn't say "funny man". I enjoyed being provocative, getting a reaction from someone. This was most evident in some of my off-color jokes, clever comments or back of the classroom jibes.

One day, I said something inappropriate, but what I considered to be extremely mild. Later, someone mentioned they thought my comment was scandalous.

Scandalous? Seriously? It was just a joke. He then informed me that by making that statement, other people could incorrectly assume that I approved of the behavior that I stated in my "joke" See, I thought scandal was more akin to flouting an extramarital relationship or intentionally doing something wrong. So, I looked up the definition:

"A circumstance or action that offends propriety or established moral conceptions or disgraces those associated with it."[1]

Wow. At the time, I belonged to an accountability group and approached one of my close friends and shared the story. He relayed how he tried to avoid even the potential for someone to misinterpret his behavior. For example, he doesn't ride alone with a woman who is not his wife or daughter in the car because someone might misconstrue the situation.

Remember Bad Bill? (Stage Seven) His friends outside of church did not know he was striving for spiritual growth. He realized if he was going to be Catholic, he had to "be" Catholic. He had to "clean up his act". He stopped telling dirty jokes. He quit the put-downs. He averted his eyes when he knew what he saw would create bad thoughts.

Being a selfless Catholic means worrying less about what others think about you and more about how you can positively affect them. As a consequence of this, over time, you often change your thoughts from assuming the worst in people, to assuming the best.

Wait a minute. Doesn't that make me a sap? An easy mark? Maybe. Let's say you are driving down the road and a car pulls out in front of you. You scream out loud, "You stupid jerk". You think what an idiot and bad driver that person is. You are stewing as you pull into your destination. The question you have to ask yourself is, did that person even know they pulled out in front of you? Or, if they knew, did they realize there wasn't enough space but had to keep going? Or, did they get a call that their child was hurt and they were focused on getting to the hospital as soon as possible? It could be almost any of those reasons but most likely it wasn't to ruin your day. You chose to assume it was about you. You made a mental decision to think the worst. Why not think the best? **Stage Fifteen is about learning to forgive and accept others.**

I once worked with a priest who was in charge of an order of priests. I went to complain to him about the behavior of one of his priests, specifically some negative comments he had made. When I finished my litany, the superior looked at me and said, "Oh, I am sure he didn't mean it that way."

I looked at him incredulously, and said something like, "No. Father, he did". The priest would have none of it. I left there confused, Did he not see the behavior? Was he covering for the other priest?

As I reflected on this over time, I realized that the priest in charge chose to think the best of people. In fact, at this stage in his formation, the "good" was his instinctual response. I couldn't even fathom that one could become so holy as to be that charitable.

What did it cost this priest to be "bamboozled"? Worst case, the offending priest erred. His superior may have concluded that as an adult, the priest is responsible for his own behavior and for amending himself. If he deliberately did something, the superior might have felt that I was the one to deal with it versus him, since it would be hearsay for him to try to resolve. Or, he might have known something was happening to the priest which affected his judgment—he may have been suffering from depression, for example.

It was more likely that the priest in charge knew the offending priest was a little of a hothead. But he also knew the offending priest was good at heart. He saw the love of God in him. He chose to let that be his view of the offending priest.

Does that mean he shouldn't act on it? No, if there were a variety of complaints or occurrences that he perceived, it is incumbent upon him to follow up. And I am sure that he would.

For the reasons mentioned above, we often judge people. Why do we do that? It partially fills that hole of insecurity. Making fun of someone mistakenly makes us think better of ourselves. "Will you look at that?

She is wearing plaid with stripes. I am glad I have better taste than her."

I used to measure my wife against my strengths. (Of course, that way I always won!) And besides, who cares about empathy, kindness and unconditional love? (Her strengths.)

Sometimes, we are so self-focused, we don't put ourselves into others' shoes, as my priest friend above did.

How does one become others-oriented?

One, we can recognize that God told us to be this way. "Jesus makes charity the new commandment. By loving his own "to the end," he makes manifest the Father's love, which he receives. By loving one another, the disciples imitate the love of Jesus, which they themselves receive. When Jesus says: "As the Father has loved me, so have I loved you; abide in my love." and again: "This is my commandment, that you love one another as I have loved you."[2]

How admirable the plan, the universal law laid down by Providence, that it is through men, that men are to find out the way to salvation.[3]

Two, we know that performing these acts pleases Him and that He will assist us if we pray for courage, strength and patience. "And thus, O Jesus, my indirect union with You through my works, that is my relations, according to Your will, with creatures, will become the sequel to my direct union with You through mental prayer, the liturgical life, and the sacraments... But since it is in obedience to You that I do so these objects to which I have to give my attention becomes the means willed by You to achieve my union with You."[4]

And three, we review our actions in our daily examination. Our desire is to change our heart toward people and accept them with all of their peculiarities and faults... just like you accept yourself.

Forgiving and accepting others

Why is there so much talk in the Bible about judgment and forgiveness? Heck, even "Our Father" has "forgive[n] us our trespasses as we forgive those who trespass against us."

Obviously, being critical of others, gossiping, and harboring resentment, are modern problems, not unique to you!

The following quote from Russian author Fyodor Dostoevsky in The Brothers Karamazov, describes, reassuringly, the human condition:

"I love humanity... but I can't help being surprised at myself: the more I love humanity in general, the less I love men in particular, I mean, separately, as separate individuals. In my dreams... I am very often passionately determined to save humanity, and I might quite likely have sacrificed my life for my fellow-creatures, if for some reason it has been suddenly demanded of me, and yet I'm quite incapable of living with anyone in one room for two days together, and I know that from experience. As soon as anyone comes close to me, his personality begins to oppress my vanity and restrict my freedom. I'm capable of hating the best men in twenty-four hours: one because he sits too long over his dinner, another because he has a cold in the head and keeps blowing his nose. But, on the other hand, it invariably happened that the more I hated men individually, the more ardent became my love for humanity at large."[5]

I feel better now, don't you?

Why are we that way? Why do we react to people like that? Reasons might include:

We are insecure. We often feel better about ourselves when we see something in other people we can judge—their appearance, lack of skill, ignorance. By perceiving them as worse than us, we feel better.

We are prideful. We have thoughts such as, "I don't have those problems", "He is wasting MY time. Can't he tell that I am busy / important?"

We are all self-oriented. That isn't necessarily a bad thing. We need to be for self-preservation and to enable ourselves to flourish. For instance, in reading this book, you are most likely doing some self-reflecting. That's healthy. Unfortunately, like much sin, we take a good thing and perverse it. We have too high a regard for self. Selfishness is defined in the dictionary as to be "concerned excessively or exclusively with oneself: seeking or concentrating on one's own advantage, pleasure, or well-being without regard for others."[6]

I like this definition as it shows well the excess of self-focus and self-advantage.

Often, we don't consider where others are coming from because we are so intent on our own position. We might not even be right! I have described myself as "often wrong but never in doubt". Gosh, am I so prideful that I even boast of my pride? No, it is just a realization of how flawed I am and that I need to rely on God to help me.

There is a story I once heard that reminds me I am not always right:

There was a man sitting at the gate of an airport waiting to board the plane. He had bought a small package of cookies and glanced over and saw them on the seat next to him. He picked them up, opened the bag and had one. He then put the bag back on the seat.

A few moments later, the woman in the seat on the other side of the cookie bag, reached over, picked up the bag, and took out a cookie and ate it! The man was incensed, but didn't say anything. A minute later he reached over and had another, and a couple of minutes later, the woman took another cookie. He thought, "The gall of this woman". He was steaming, but since he was trying to not create a scene he continued to sit quietly. The boarding call then sounded, the woman picked up the bag, looked inside and saw there were two cookies left. She tipped the bag to the man to have a cookie, he took it and then she finished the last cookie.

He walked onto the plane just steaming. As he buckled his seatbelt he thought, "What a terrible person. How could she do that? Has she no shame?"

He then opened up his briefcase and to his surprise, noticed that his bag of cookies was still inside his briefcase and he realized he'd been eating hers.

Regardless of why, we need to change the way we think about others. "We need to accept people just as they are, understand that their approach and values are not the same as ours, and to broaden our minds and soften our hearts to them... We must learn to renounce the pride that we take in being right, which often prevents us from entering into the other person's thoughts."[7]

As you can guess, that's a tall order. Maybe that is why there is so much reference to forgiveness and not judging in the bible.

"Not judging another takes empathy, the ability to understand and the ability to share the feelings of another person. Developing empathy is crucial for establishing relationships and behaving compassionately."[8]

Candidly, it is very difficult for me to not be critical of people. Lately, I have been working on "shredding judgement". By that I mean whenever I observe something that I deem "wrong" with someone or whenever they say or do something that I might judge, I try to eliminate that thought. I recognize how trifling being judgmental is. It doesn't help anyone move forward. Yes, it may feed my pride but it actually gets in the way of my interaction with that individual. I certainly am not thinking of how I can be Christ to them. I now try to put aside my judgment and focus on what the person is trying to communicate to me and how I can contribute with charity to this interaction.

God invites us to accept others in the same way we accept ourselves— as flawed, imperfect beings who are completely loved by God. Many challenges with others occur due to miscommunication or misunderstanding. A key moment occurs when we recognize we might not always be right, or at least that the other person may be looking at an issue from a different, not wrong, perspective.

I think a great way in which God gets us to mitigate our pride is through our own faults and deficiencies. We are reminded of our weaknesses and through this, hopefully, we become less judgmental of others. We can either learn from it or make an excuse. This is an ongoing, and humbling, exercise.

You might say, I understand what you are saying about not judging, but what about forgiving someone who wronged you? We must react in exactly the same way! Now, this is not to say we don't protect ourselves from abuse, or occasionally confront the person who hurt us, but in the end, "we need to learn to forgive other people for making us suffer or disappointing us, and even to accept the problems that they create for us as graces and blessings. This attitude is neither spontaneous or natural, but it is the only one by which to achieve peace and interior freedom."[9]

Reflection

1. Why do you judge others? How does it make you feel? Why is that important to you?
2. In looking at others can you see things from their perspective? Can you put yourself in their shoes?
3. Can you accept they have different temperaments, skills, flaws and attitudes than you, and that isn't right or wrong?
4. What emotions do you feel when you are hurt by someone else?
5. Do you think it is possible you might have misinterpreted the situation? That they perhaps weren't thinking about you but about their own feelings?
6. If you conclude that they deliberately hurt you, what process can you go through to forgive them?

MAKING THE COMMITMENT
TO BE "ALL-IN"
Stage Sixteen

There is a term in Texas, "Hold 'em, Poker", where you take all of your money and put it in the pot. If you lose, you lose it all. Up to that point you might have painstakingly made a little here, lost a little there, slowly building your stack of chips (or cash). And then, you have a hand that feels so good you want to bet it all. Then you go, "all-in". It is a scary yet exhilarating time.

God is waiting for us to go "all-in". He is there to help us not only place the bet but win the hand and win the game! We just have to make the commitment.

But we hesitate. We think, "If I go all-in, I can never have too much to drink again. I won't be invited to parties and if I am, I won't have any fun." We might think, "If I go all-in, I won't be able to say something inappropriate. People think I am funny and I will just become a holy roller", and "If I go all-in, I will have to be honest all of the time. It might affect how much money I can make". Those are just some of the thoughts we might have in the first two minutes!

The devil doesn't want us to go all-in because with God, we have a better hand. The devil feeds our fear. He has us doubt ourselves: "I just can't do it", "I don't want to do it!" He makes it into this huge decision. And it is. But with God, if you make a mistake, you don't lose it all.

I remember trying to make this decision. I loved God. I wanted to be good. I was afraid, but mostly, I didn't feel I was good enough. I didn't feel that I COULD be good enough. And then it hit me. I don't have to do this all on my own. Jesus will help me. Right then, I said in my mind, "Ok, Lord, you want this. I want this. But I can't do it without you. I might mess up. I need you to forgive my failings and sins, and to help me persevere.

Immediately, I felt relaxed. God was on the hook with me. I remember the joy I had in thinking, "I am all in for Jesus." I still have that joy.

But I still mess up. Intellectually, I have given myself totally to God. But my humanness, my concupiscence, hinders me in its execution. Blessed Columba Marmion wrote this to a Carmelite nun: "It is much easier to say to our Lord, 'I give myself to you without reserve' than to do so in reality."[1]

Thank goodness for confession. We are not perfect creatures. God is not looking for perfection. He is looking for an abandonment to divine providence.

Blessed Mamion states again, " It is not our perfection which is to dazzle God... no, it is our misery, our wretchedness avowed which draws down his mercy."[2]

Being aware that we are nothing without God is a tall order. Our humanness gets in the way. Nonetheless, what does it mean to be "all in"? What changes within our attitude and behavior? Being "all in" means you give yourself completely to God. You recognize you have been fighting God most of the time and that surrender will bring peace and joy. You have the faith that God exists and wants the best for you, the hope that He will help you and provide for you and give you the love to act confidently. This helps you want to understand and do God's will each and every moment of every day. **Stage Sixteen is about committing to be all in.**

Easy to say. How do you do that?

Faith helps us to know God. By hope we trust in Him that by trying to be faithful we will be choosing the best path. Charity unites us to Him and compels us to act. These three virtues are the specific virtues of the life of a union with God; being constantly exercised, they inevitably grow and increase until they lead to perfection.

As mentioned before, faith, hope and love form a certain circular process. The stronger your faith, the more you hope, the more you can love, which in turn, converts your heart to create more faith.

You are now bathed in God. By that I mean, you think about God during the day, you might pray before business meetings, before tough discussions with others, or even while decision making. You truly want to live for the glory of God. God is integral in your life. But there is still sin.

You are also introspective. Controlling one's interior life requires prayer, effort, humility, patience and self-forgiveness. If it is sinful behavior, it also requires reconciliation. One challenge here is that things you thought you had under control, all of a sudden re-emerge and get you. Other areas never seem to get better. Pride tends to take you off guard. I think many of the "you do not know the hour or day" parables are meant for people trying to clean up their thoughts.

Committing to be all in involves a lot of restraint—not saying something, eliminating bad thoughts as soon as they pop into your head. We slowly begin to make instantaneous decisions about thoughts and actions that keep us on the straight and narrow.

You are working on your thought life. You have an effective examination of conscience. Humility is also critical in objectively looking at yourself and identifying areas to change and being willing to change.

Unfortunately, sometimes you'll still choose to sin. It may be a reaction, you yell at your children because you are tired and they did something inappropriate. It may also be intentional. You are tempted and you give in. God knows we are weak. God knows we need purification. God gave us confession.

Confession. It's good for the soul

Why wait until almost the end of a book about spiritual growth to bring up confession? Heck, you received the sacrament in second grade, for heaven's sake. While confession, or reconciliation, is important when you are at an earlier stage in your faith journey, it becomes central to your faith journey as you go deeper. You look forward to confession (seriously!) It is an important part of your spiritual plan.

I remember, when I was younger, not wanting to go to confession. Part of the reason for that was the loathing to come clean and openly admit my sins. Part of the reason was not understanding the point. What's the big deal? God knows I was sorry. Yet, I always felt better when I went. I think I was more relieved than anything.

As we go deeper there is a greater sense of connection with our thought life. You perform more in the moment through self-examination and correction, and you have a desire to be sinless. They are all part of your "improvement ecosystem".

Confession is a sacrament so it brings grace to strengthen us for the journey, the battle, and not simply the forgiveness of our sins alone.

 Conversion is accomplished in daily life by gestures of reconciliation, concern for the poor, the exercise and defense of justice and right, by the admission of faults to one's brethren, fraternal correction, revision of life, examination of conscience, spiritual direction, acceptance of suffering, endurance of persecution for the sake of righteousness. Taking up one's cross each day and following Jesus is the surest way of penance."[3]

YOU LIVE YOUR LIFE, not in a hyper-analytical mode but simply by trying to live in the moment—trying to be obedient and actually wanting to be obedient because it brings you joy. There is almost relief in knowing that when you make a mistake, there is confession. So you boldly march forward!

"For by grace you have been saved through faith, and this is not from you; it is the gift of God; it is not from works, so no one may boast."[4]

Reflection

1. What is keeping you from being "all-in"?
2. What are you afraid of?
3. Is confession a regular part of your relationship with God?
4. What do you need to do to trust God to help you?
5. Can you make the commitment now to go all in?

EVANGELIZING CATHOLIC
Stage Seventeen

Nothing scares the average Catholic more than being asked to evangelize! The very word sends shivers down their spines. Or so it seems. I remember asking a friend how she thought she could evangelize. She backed up, looked at me in a panic and said, "I can't knock on doors like the Mormons."

Recognize I didn't say go door to door, but that's how she thought she should evangelize. Not surprisingly, this is a common reaction. Many Catholics think the only way to evangelize is by being a "bible thumper". Unfortunately, as that is what they see as the only way to evangelize, they don't feel inspired to do it.

Yet, Jesus said very specifically: "Brothers and sisters, consider this: whoever sows sparingly will also reap sparingly, and whoever sows bountifully will also reap bountifully. Each must do as already determined, without sadness or compulsion, for God loves a cheerful giver. Moreover, God is able to make every grace abundant for you, so that in all things, always having all you need, you may have an abundance for every good work."[1]

In other words, no excuses. We are called to say yes to God and we are called to evangelize. Jesus' last words on earth were: "Go to all nations and baptize them..."[2]

In my faith journey, I must admit I was hesitant to turn my life over to Christ for fear that He would have me be a missionary to Africa. Seriously. With some trepidation, I told God I wanted to do his will, and be "all in". Several years went by and Julie and I went to Ghana to visit a priest friend who had been recalled back to his home country. We went to spiritually fill him up and have an adventure. On the last day of our visit the priest surprised us with a meeting where he asked us to help him build a Catholic High School. At that time I was familiar with fundraising for schools. After discussing this with friends in the US, we said yes. This last year we completed a school that educates 800 students. In retrospect, God DID send me to Africa to evangelize. Just not in the way I had feared.

God has given you certain skills, temperaments and experiences. He did that for a reason. Most likely, He will have you utilize those strengths in executing His will. If you trust Him, He will provide all you need to see you through.

Nonetheless, God doesn't call us to be successful. He calls us to be faithful. While all things work together for good, going through the effort, and failing, might build the necessary virtue for your holiness or for your next task.

Ways to evangelize

The number one way to prepare to evangelize is to have a fruitful interior life. Persuasive arguments, pleadings or promises have done far less in convincing people to become Catholic, or a more devout Catholic, than the influence radiated by a soul united with Christ.

The more a soul is united with Christ, the more others see that in your demeanor and feel your sincerity and love. People will see the truth, beauty and goodness in you and be drawn to it.

In calling you to evangelize, God will use your temperament, if you let Him! Most people are not called to stand on a podium and preach. (That must be reassuring to the introverts reading this.) Prayer and sacrifice are the most efficacious means of evangelizing. Anyone can do this.

You might feel ill one day and choose to offer it up for a change of heart for a relative. You might pray nightly for a holy marriage for your children. Or, you might offer up not eating dinner one night for those struggling with addiction. People you don't even know! You are becoming more and more outside yourself and wish the beauty of being in the kingdom of heaven on all people.

The best example I can think of in exercising prayer and sacrifice together is cloistered religious people who spend a good part of every day in isolation, praying for others. They selflessly have dedicated their lives to praying for priests, peace, general conversion of souls, and so on. What a beautiful testimony from these "invisible" people.

One of the most frequent prayer requests for Catholics is for a non-practicing family member to come back to the Church. I think that happens because you have tried everything and, well, you can't "push a rope." No one is going to come to Christ as a result of being lectured or having been forced them to read books (except this book, of course!) They have to choose. Instead of it being your job to bring them to the faith, ask God to do it. He will soften their hearts, touch their souls and give them opportunities to choose Him.

You might be saying you do pray for others but you also want to do something active without being completely freaked out! That makes sense—you have grown with love for God and want to please Him. Additionally, you genuinely love others to the extent you want to do something for them. "The love of Christ compels us."[3]

Don't worry. You don't have to do public speaking, make cold calls, sleep on mats, bathe the sick and elderly, fundraise, perform great works or move to Africa to be considered an evangelist. However, you might be asked to step outside of your comfort zone.

At this point in your journey, I am assuming you are doing a fair amount of volunteering and personal spiritual development activities. This stage might provide you with an opportunity to go deeper. First, pray for God to help you discern how He might want to use you. Next, think about what talents you have and what types of activities you might make a bigger impact in. They may be areas you are already volunteering in. If you are in a bible study, volunteer to be a table leader. If you work with areas that have new volunteers, offer to be a mentor. Or, start a new ministry! Be part of the senior team of an apostolate.

If you are a little more daring, you can try volunteering with mission trips, manning a homeless shelter, working with a prison ministry or St. Vincent de Paul.

If you are new to volunteering, I suggest you dip your toe into it. Don't make a long term commitment but try out several options first and see what resonates with you or that you feel called to. You will be surprised at what you can do. You will be overjoyed by how you feel afterwards in helping those in need physically and spiritually. You will be amazed at how working with others in an apostolate brings both mentor and beginner closer to God.

Reflection

1. How are you called to work in the vineyard?
2. What role in evangelization do you feel you could do?
3. What's stopping you from going deeper?

BEING "ALL-IN"
Stage Eighteen

The timeframe for going from *committing* to be all in to *being* all in can be measured in years. **Stage Eighteen is about learning to become detached and exercising abandonment.** We are creating habits and those take time. Do not despair. God is helping us along the way.

One place in which you will notice a change is your thought life. It's no longer just a matter of not saying something. It's not about not thinking things either or if sinful thoughts pop up, dismissing them immediately, not as an act of the will but as an effect of habit.

Let's say you are talking to a friend and he says something negative about someone else and without hesitation you say, "oh gosh, let's not go there", and the conversation pivots. Later you realize that at the time, you didn't even think of why you said that. You stop and give glory to God. You are grateful for your charity that God has bestowed on you. Being all-in drives more and more habitual action toward the good.

All-in Catholics strive for holiness and the desire to do God's will. Without question, along the way there are pitfalls, errors in judgement and sinful behavior. That's called being human. In these cases you immediately beg God for forgiveness, you right any wrong that you have created or even participated in, and you commit to not sin again. You go to confession purposefully.

Being "all in" is about selfless awareness of God and it results in service to others. We want them to experience the joy of Christ.

How do you live this life in a world that promotes promiscuity, violence and anti-Catholic behavior? How do you become a beacon of light even though it is counter cultural? How do you react when you are chastised for your beliefs? How do you even have a conversation with someone who fervently believes in relativism?

It is challenging. You can trust God. You might try to be so filled up with Christ that you are impervious to the insults, the inconsiderate actions and the lack of charity of others. In fact, you seek out where they are coming from so you can be Christ to them. They may not always respond positively, but you can! With God as the focus, with God as the person you are doing things for, you will build strength and even joy in interactions with others. How? Detachment and abandonment.

Detachment and abandonment

In Stage Six, I talked about the theological virtues and the synergy of faith building hope, hope building love, love strengthening faith, ad infinitum. In my earlier stages of faith I didn't realize how intertwined these three virtues really are. Let me explain.

If you have a strong faith in God, you not only believe in Him but you also believe in His goodness, His ability and His willingness to impact your life. Having this immense faith enables hope to flourish in trusting that He WILL do or provide what is right for you, and that you will lovingly act.

"If we leave everything to God, He will do all that is necessary for our holiness." [1]

I think this is a big step. I had to logically come to grips with the fact God has not only given me everything that I am and have but also has provided the tools, people and experiences for me to continue to grow in faith, hope and love. So, why not trust Him to lead me if I abandon my will? I realize this is easier said than done.

So, (God the) Father knows best! Since He will lead you in the right direction, you can trust that the outcome you receive is the best outcome for you. This is called abandonment, that is, the abandonment of self to the will of God. Since God is the only good, you must detach yourself from any love of created things. How?

> *If we carefully fulfill the duties imposed on us by our state of life, if we quietly follow any impulse coming from God, if we peacefully submit to the influence of grace, we are making an act of total abandonment.*"[2]

YOU HAVE INTELLECTUALLY CONCLUDED that God has the right plan for you. You actively try to be detached. It is your act of love and obedience of turning over all things to God, that God desires. In return, you will receive graces of fulfillment and joy. Sometimes you will be successful, sometimes not. In my life there is still a huge desire to steer the ship. I continually need to actively let go. Yet, if you persevere, you will be more confident in trusting in Him, all the while growing in love.

Even our failures may be part of God's plan. Remember my story about not getting into medical school? At the time I was devastated. Now what do I think? God may have wanted me to try, fail, and learn something in the process. So I should not fret. I should not be discouraged. Neither should you.

You can have faith that He has something better for you in mind, so you can accept the loss, or more correctly, you accept what you perceive as a loss. God has a plan.

Therefore, your faith is the foundation for your hope. "The more perplexing the situation, the more you can hope for a happy solution. The heart says, 'All will be well. God has the matter in hand. You need fear nothing.'"[3]

Your hope, then, which is grounded in faith, causes you to act in love. You are obedient, and you are rewarded. When God finds a soul emptied of self, he fills it with His love. He provides a joy that radiates and builds more faith. And the circle continues.

Reflection

1. In which areas have you shown improvement over the years? What did you have to do to make those changes happen? Take time to thank God for this personal growth.
2. What improvements are you currently working on and how are you working on them? What might you do to be more successful? Pray to God now for guidance to help in these areas.
3. Are you being comfortable or are you reaching out to evangelize? Are you involved in charitable works?

IN UNION WITH GOD
Stage Nineteen

S tage Nineteen is about living in Union with God. Union with God means that all of your activities and thoughts are in sync with God's will. It is the epitome of unselfishness. Your joyful obedience to God's will is made possible by your deep love and gratitude creating your desire to please Him. It seems like a pretty tall order. It is. Nonetheless, God created you to achieve this end by striving to be the best version of yourself that you can be. He gave you the tools as described in this book. He reaches out to you incessantly.

The difference between being all-in and reaching this stage is that you are no longer trying to steer. This is why the daily examination of conscience is so important. You try to discern God's will for each day, and for your actions and decisions throughout that day. You still have your station in life so you must perform the duties of that state. (God would never tell you to abandon your responsibilities. That is the first check if your discernment is God's will.) While trying to achieve the objectives in the day's plan, you accept any outcome as a means of God working to bring good to a situation.

Yes, you take the necessary steps to achieve the goals, yet you don't have an inordinate desire for success. You subjugate your will such that "God's will be done". He has a better plan. This faith and trust allows you to execute your activities with hope and love, joyfully!

You have read about all of these stages in the journey to a union with God and you have traversed many of them in your search for Him. You have hopefully identified where you are on the path and have come up with means to reach the next stage. This is a life-long process. Some things might seem like a burden now, but they will become second nature in the future. The end stage may seem overwhelming now but focus on the practical next steps within your reach. Thankfully, God is there the entire time. He sends you graces during prayers, during reception of the sacraments and while you are carrying out ordinary activities of life. You will be reinforced in faith. You will be more confident in your hope for the future and your love will spur you on.

While you may not reach union with God in this life, you may achieve snippets of perfection. Times of joy. Times of serenity knowing that, for this specific moment, you are in union with God.

You don't have to give into the lies and shortcuts that the world promises. When you walk out your door you can be joyful, not defensive or afraid. You have Christ! You have the pearl of great price! While not boasting, haughty or prideful, you can show by example that you live the life that others want. You have accepted your nothingness. You are God's.

Keeping your spiritual tank filled

Even joyful people get tired. Sometimes your own humanness gets in the way via disappointment, overcommitment, miscommunication, doubt, and a myriad of other human frailties. Therefore, it is important for you to seek opportunities to fill up your spiritual gas tank. Besides prayer, the sacraments, and adoration, it is very helpful to have other devout Catholics who strengthen you, affirm you and even hold you accountable. Besides a spiritual director, you might get involved with men's or women's accountability groups, frequent fellowship with others or especially get-togethers with other faithful families and share the joy and challenges. Seek out these relationships to wallow in the joy of Christ.

A challenge for many Catholics is the difficulty in saying no. It is important to reflect on what you can actually commit to in order to be both effective and healthy. A good examination regarding first your duties to your state in life, then your other activities, is essential to becoming a good, long term evangelizer.

At every stage there may be impediments to joy. You might simply feel tired. You might be tempted, you might get caught up in accomplishment versus simply doing the will of God. Step back in prayer. Take time to thank Jesus for that which He has done for you. Be grateful. Meet with others on your team. Ask God for guidance. Spend time in front of the Blessed Sacrament or receive Jesus in the Eucharist. Be joyful in knowing that "God doesn't ask that we succeed in everything, but that we are faithful. However beautiful our work may be, let us not become attached to it. Always remain prepared to give it up, without losing your peace."[1]

Thank you for your faith, your desire, your efforts and your example in pursuing the kingdom of heaven.

Reflection

1. Congratulations, you have finished the book. Which stage you are at? Decide on a next step.
2. If you haven't created a Plan of Life, create one. What commitments are you going to make to your Plan of Life?
3. How will you maintain balance between your state of life, your apostolic work and being spiritually filled up so that you can work in the vineyard?
4. How do you plan to share this message with others?

NOTES

Preface

1. St. Francis De Sales, *Introduction to the Devout Life.* (Rochford: *Tan Books, 1994)*, p. 3

The Goal: Joy

1. Luke 17:21 New American Bible.
2. Psalm 16:11.
3. "Joy" Theopedia, https://www.theopedia.com/joy (Viewed 8/8/2021.)
4. Pope St John Paul, Closing of World Youth Day, Homily Of The Holy Father John Paul II, vatican.va. (Aug. 9th, 2000.) https://www.vatican.va/content/john-paul-ii/en/homilies/2000/documents/hf_jp-ii_hom_20000820_gmg.html (Viewed 9/22/2021.)
5. Matt 6:33.
6. "The Passion of Saints Perpetua and Felicity, 203 AD." Fordham University, https://sourcebooks.fordham.edu/source/perpetua.asp (Viewed 9/22/2021.)
7. "Saint Lawrence", Franciscan Media, https://www.franciscanmedia.org/saint-of-the-day/saint-lawrence (Viewed 1/31/21.)
8. Luke 23:43.
9. John, 10:10.
10. Mark, 12:30.

Stage 2: Seeking God

1. Plato, Plato: Five Dialogues: Euthyphro, Apology, Crito, Meno, Phaedo. Indianapolis: Hacket Publishing (2002) p. 41.
2. Saint Augustine, *Confessions.* New York: Oxford University Press, (2008) p. 3.
3. John 6:60, 66.
4. Rick Warren, *The Purpose Driven Life.* Grand Rapids: Zondervan, (2002) p. 148.
5. The fight-or-flight response is a physiological reaction that occurs in response to a perceived harmful event, attack, or threat to survival. It was first described by Walter Bradford Cannon. His theory states that animals react to threats with a general discharge of the sympathetic nervous system, preparing the animal for fighting or fleeing. More specifically, the adrenal medulla produces a hormonal cascade that results in the secretion of [hormones]. Wikipedia 2/14/21.
6. Erich Fromm. *The Art of Loving.* New York: Harper and Row (1956) p. 120-121.
7. St. Thomas Aquinas, "Question 161 Humility." Summa Theologica, https://www.newadvent.org/summa/3161.htm. (Viewed 9/22/2021.)
8. St. Augustine, Letters. 118, NewAdvent.org , https://www.newadvent.org/fathers/1102118.htm p. 22. (Viewed 9/22/2021).

Stage 3: On the Fence

1. Luke, 10:27.
2. St. Edith Stein,. *Edith Stein Essays on Woman*, Washington DC: ICS Publications (2012) p. 8
3. St. John Damascus, "De Fide Orthodoxa: An Exact Exposition Of The Orthodox Faith", *Patrologia Græca*, Paris: Imprimerie Catholique, 1857-1866, p. 94.
4. "Prayer" USCCB website, https://www.usccb.org/prayer-and-worship/prayers-and-devotions/prayers. (Viewed 1/11/21.)
5. Catechism of the Catholic Church. New York, Doubleday, (1994) 2697.
6. For a more detailed explanation on these three types of prayer, please go to the Appendix Exhibit II.
7. Ibid 2702-2703.
8. Ibid 2702-2703.
9. De Sales, p. 59.
10. Blessed Columba Marmion, *"Union with God"*. Bethesda: Zaccheus Press (2006), p.59.
11. Catechism 2761.
12. CS Lewis, "The Efficacy of Prayer, Inchristus. https://inchristus.com/wp-content/uploads/2011/05/efficacy-of-prayer-cslewis.pdf. (Viewed 9/22/2021.)

Stage 4: Develop a Love Relationship With God

1. Dr. Jeff Mallinson, "What are Goodness, Truth and Beauty?" The jaggedword.com (Jan 28 2016) https://thejaggedword.com/2016/01/28/what-are-goodness-truth-and-beauty/ (Viewed 08/08/21.)
2. Catechism. 2500.
3. Adolphe Tanquerey SS DD, *The Spiritual Life*, 2nd Edition. Charlotte: Tan Books (2000) p. 568.

Stage 6: Church-Going Catholic… Maybe

1. John Ruskin, "The Crown of Wild Olive: Three Lectures on Work, Traffic, and War", University of California Libraries (1866).
2. Catechism. 1996.
3. February 21, 2016 by Rev. McCartney https://www.stmarysroslyn.com/pastors_page/?p=248 (Viewed 3/31/21.)
4. Philippians 4:8.
5. Catechism. 1803.
6. Matt 7:5.
7. Catechism. 1817-1818, 1820.
8. "Love Is the Greatest of The Theological Virtues", CatholicTherapists.com, https://www.catholictherapists.com/articles/love-is-the-greatest-of-the-theological-virtues (Viewed July 30, 2021.)
9. Ephesians 2:8-9.

Stage 7: Being a Sunday Catholic

1. Fr. John Bartunek, LC. "How Can I Identify My Root Sin?" Spiritual Direction.com, 4/26/2010. https://spiritualdirection.com/2010/04/26/how-can-i-identify-my-root-sin. (Viewed 1/13/21.)

Stage 8: I Want to be a Better Person, a Better Catholic

1. Jacques Philippe, "Interior Freedom". New York. (Sept, 2007), p 10.
2. Thomas Kempis, *The Imitation of Christ*, Mineola:Dover Publications (2003), p 28.
3. Romans 12:2.
4. Philippe, p. 35.
5. Ibid, p. 39.
6. Ibid, p. 39.

Stage 9: The Struggle Between Heart, Mind and Soul

1. Catechism, 1263, 1264.
2. St. Augustine, p. 104.
3. Oscar Wilde, *Lady Windermere's Fan*. Penguin Popular Classics. New York. (1995). Spoiler Alert: It didn't end well for him.
4. 2 Corinthians, 12:7-9.
5. 2 Corinthians, 12:7.
6. Tanquerey, P. 503
7. Hebrews 5:8-9
8. St. Francis De Sales, p. 255
9. Marmion, p. 30.

Stage 10: Committed Catholic

1. Pope St. John Paul II, "Novo Millennio Ineunte." https://www.vatican.va/content/john-paul-ii/en/apost_letters/2001/documents/hf_jp-ii_apl_20010106_novo-millennio-ineunte.html, 2001. p. 1. (viewed 9/18/2021.)
2. Mark, 1:15.
3. 1 Corinthians, 11:28–31.

Stage 11: Conforming the Inside With the Outside

1. "Spiritual Direction." https://www.catholicspiritualdirection.org. (Viewed 1/31/2021.)
2. Fr. John Bartunek, Catholic Exchange. https://catholicexchange.com/what-are-the-key-characteristics-of-good-spiritual-direction (Viewed 2/19/21.)

Stage 12: Getting Rid of the Old Self

1. Tanquerey, p. 364.
2. Ibid, p. 362.
3. Catechism, 1434.
4. Matthew, 6:1-15.
5. Pope Paul VI "Mysterium Fidei." vatican.va. https://www.vatican.va/content/paul-vi/en/encyclicals/documents/hf_p-vi_enc_03091965_mysterium.html p. 67. (Viewed 9/21/2021.)
6. Fr. Raoul Plus, SJ, *Progress in Divine Union*. Manchester. Sophia (2004) p. 19.
7. Ibid, p. 37.

Stage 14: Spiritual Dryness

1. Ibid, p.100.
2. Ibid, p. 98.
3. Philippe, p. 49.
4. Ibid, p. 51.
5. Ibid, p. 58.

Stage 15: Being Others-Oriented

1. Merriam-Webster, "Scandal." https://www.merriam-webster.com/dictionary/scandal. (Viewed 8/9/2021.)
2. Catechism, 1836.
3. Jean-Baptiste Chautard, OCSO, *Soul of the Apostolate*. Charlotte, Tan Books. (2012) p. 5.
4. Ibid, p. 274.
5. Fyodor Dostoevsky, *The Brothers Karamazov*. Barnes and Noble Classics, New York. (2004) p. 61.
6. Merriam Webster, "selfish" https://www.merriam-webster.com/dictionary/selfish. (Viewed 3/11/21.)
7. Philippe, p. 62.
8. Psychology Today, "Empathy." https://www.psychologytoday.com/us/basics/empathy. (Viewed 3/11/21.)
9. Philippe, p. 61.

Stage 16: Making the Commitment to Be All-In

1. Marmion, p. 64.
2. Ibid, p. 99.
3. Catechism, 1435.
4. Ephesians, 2:8-9.

Stage 17: Evangelizing Catholic

1. 2 Corinthians, 9:6-10.
2. Matthew, 28:19.
3. 2 Corinthians, 5:14.

Stage 18: Being All-In

1. Jean-Pierre De Caussade, *Abandonment to Divine Providence*. Doubleday, New York. (1975) p. 40.
2. Ibid, p. 66.
3. Ibid, p. 101.

Stage 19: In Union With God

1. Mother Teresa, *The Joy in Loving: A Guide to Daily Living*. Penguin Compass, New York. 2000) p.

Exhibit III: The Apostles' and Nicene Creeds

1. Catechism, 194-195.
2. Catechism, 197.

Exhibit IV: Transubstantiation

1. John 60, 66-68.

ACKNOWLEDGMENTS

Writing a book is humbling.

You ask yourself, is it good? Will anyone read it? Does this chapter get the point across? Heck, does this chapter even make sense? With that in mind, I want to share my sincere thanks to those who read the material, made suggestions and encouraged me throughout this process: Scott and Regina Brun, Fr. Ryan Richardson, Deacon Derek Gant, Greg Palen, Earl Pizzarelli, Naoise Johnston, Paula Gondek and with special thanks to Allen Hunt, who reviewed the early drafts and helped me craft the narrative. And to Julie for her rock steady faith and support of this and all of my off-the-wall projects. Thank you all for your love and support.

About the Author

Tom Clements is a cradle Catholic who has been on a circuitous path on his journey of faith. He has gone from daily communicant and altar boy, to spending several years going to the nondenominational "Church of the Open Door". When he found that unfulfilling, he returned to the Catholic Church as a Sunday Catholic, from which he began a decades-long immersion into deepening his relationship with God, becoming "all in" and flirting with being in Union with God.

Tom has had great ups and down in his life and, while he owned his own company and had a beautiful family, he still felt unfulfilled. He turned to God and hasn't looked back. This book relies on the "Deposit of Faith" to construct a personal pathway for readers to become joyful.

More about Tom:

- He started, and was able to sell one of the first Intranet companies in the USA in 1999
- He started the first Catholic College in Georgia in 2001. SCC graduated two classes and educated over 200 students
- He spearheaded the founding and construction of a thriving 800-strong residential Catholic High School in Ghana, Africa
- He spent the last 20 years volunteering, being a major donor, and being an employee of multiple non-profits resulting in his writing a successful book called, "How to Run a Nonprofit" and consulting worldwide
- He's been a keynote speaker to groups of 10-1500 giving his testimony as well as encouraging others to get outside of themselves to participate in "loving thy neighbor"

You can email Tom at Tom.thepath2joy@gmail.com
Or visit his website: www.thepath2joy.com

APPENDIX

Exhibit I

The Litany of Humility

Lord Jesus. Meek and humble of heart, Hear me.

From the desire of being esteemed, Deliver me, Jesus.

From the desire of being loved, Deliver me, Jesus.

From the desire of being extolled, Deliver me, Jesus.

From the desire of being honored, Deliver me, Jesus.

From the desire of being praised, Deliver me, Jesus.

From the desire of being preferred to others, Deliver me, Jesus.

From the desire of being consulted, Deliver me, Jesus.

From the desire of being approved, Deliver me, Jesus.

From the fear of being humiliated, Deliver me, Jesus.

From the fear of being despised, Deliver me, Jesus.

From the fear of suffering rebukes, Deliver me, Jesus.

From the fear of being calumniated, Deliver me, Jesus.

From the fear of being forgotten, Deliver me, Jesus.

From the fear of being ridiculed, Deliver me, Jesus.

From the fear of being wronged, Deliver me, Jesus.

From the fear of being suspected, Deliver me, Jesus.

That others may be loved more than I, Jesus, grant me the grace to desire it.

That others may be esteemed more than I, Jesus, grant me the grace to desire it.

That, in the opinion of the world, others may increase and I may decrease, Jesus, grant me the grace to desire it.

That others may be chosen and I set aside, Jesus, grant me the grace to desire it.

That others may be praised and I unnoticed, Jesus, grant me the grace to desire it.

That others may be preferred to me in everything, Jesus, grant me the grace to desire it.

That others may become holier than I, provided that I may become as holy as I should, Jesus, grant me the grace to desire it.

— Rafael Cardinal Merry del Val (1865-1930)

Exhibit II

The Three Types of Prayer

Vocal prayer

Vocal prayer is an important element of the Christian life. It is spoken or sung, alone or with others. It could be either an established prayer like the Lord's Prayer, the Rosary and a myriad of other written prayers, or it could be a spontaneous outpouring of communication with God.

2704 Because it is external and so thoroughly human, vocal prayer is the form of prayer most readily accessible to groups.

Even interior prayer, however, cannot neglect vocal prayer. Prayer is internalized to the extent that we become aware of him "to whom we speak;" Thus vocal prayer becomes an initial form of contemplative prayer.

Meditation

2705 Meditation is above all a quest. The mind seeks to understand the why and how of the Christian life, in order to adhere to and respond to what the Lord is asking. The required attentiveness is difficult to sustain. We are usually helped by books such as the Sacred Scriptures, particularly the Gospels; holy icons; liturgical texts of the day or season; writings of the spiritual fathers; works of spirituality; the great book of creation; and that of history the page on which the "today" of God is written.

2706 To meditate on what we read helps us to make it our own by confronting it with ourselves. To the extent that we are humble and faithful, we discover in meditation the movements that stir the heart and we are able to discern them. It is a question of acting truthfully in order to come into the light: "Lord, what do you want me to do?"

2707 There are as many and varied methods of meditation as there are spiritual masters. Christians owe it to themselves to develop the desire to meditate regularly, lest they come to resemble the three first kinds of soil in the parable of the sower. But a method is only a guide—the important thing is to advance, with the Holy Spirit, along the one way of prayer: Christ Jesus.

2708 Meditation engages thought, imagination, emotion, and desire. This mobilization of faculties is necessary in order to deepen our convictions of faith, prompt the conversion of our heart, and strengthen our will to follow Christ.

Contemplative prayer

2709 What is contemplative prayer? St. Teresa answers: "Contemplative prayer [oracion mental] in my opinion is nothing else than a close sharing between friends; it means taking time frequently to be alone with him who we know loves us."

Contemplative prayer seeks him "whom my soul loves." It is Jesus, and in him, the Father. We seek Him, because to desire Him is always the beginning of love, and we seek Him in that pure faith which causes us to be born of Him and to live in Him. In this inner prayer we can still meditate, but our attention is fixed on the Lord himself.

2710 The choice of the time and duration of the prayer arises from a determined will, revealing the secrets of the heart. We don't undertake contemplative prayer only when we have the time: we make time for the Lord, with the firm determination not to give up, no matter what trials and dryness we may encounter. We cannot always meditate, but we can always enter into inner prayer, independently of our health, work, or emotional states. The heart is the place from which this quest arises, in poverty and in faith.

2711 Entering into contemplative prayer is like entering into the Eucharistic liturgy: we "gather up" the heart, recollect our whole being under the prompting of the Holy Spirit, abide in the dwelling place of the Lord which we are, awaken our faith in order to enter into the presence of him who awaits us. We let our masks fall and turn our hearts back to the Lord who loves us, so as to hand ourselves over to him as an offering to be purified and transformed.

2712 Contemplative prayer is the prayer of the child of God, of the forgiven sinner who agrees to welcome the love by which he is loved and who wants to respond to it by loving even more. But he knows that the love he is returning is poured out by the Spirit in his heart, for everything is grace from God. Contemplative prayer is the poor and humble surrender to the loving will of the Father in ever deeper union with his beloved Son.

2713 Contemplative prayer is the simplest expression of the mystery of prayer. It is a gift, a grace; it can be accepted only in humility and poverty. Contemplative prayer is a covenant relationship established by God within our hearts. Contemplative prayer is a communion in which the Holy Trinity conforms man, the image of God, "to His likeness."

2714 Contemplative prayer is also the pre-eminently intense time of prayer. In it, the Father strengthens our inner being with power through His Spirit "that Christ may dwell in (our) hearts through faith" and we may be "grounded in love."

2715 Contemplation is a gaze of faith, fixed on Jesus. "I look at him and he looks at me." This is what a certain peasant of Ars used to say to his holy cure about his prayer before the tabernacle. This focus on Jesus is a renunciation of self. His gaze purifies our heart; the light of the countenance of Jesus illumines the eyes of our heart and teaches us to see everything in the light of his truth and his compassion for all men. Contemplation also turns its gaze on the mysteries of the life of Christ. Thus it learns the "interior knowledge of our Lord," the more to love him and follow him.

2716 Contemplative prayer is hearing the Word of God. Far from being passive, such attentiveness is the obedience of faith, the unconditional acceptance of a servant, and the loving commitment of a child. It participates in the "yes" of the Son become servant and the Fiat of God's lowly handmaid.

2717 Contemplative prayer is silence, the "symbol of the world to come" or "silent love". Words in this kind of prayer are not speeches; they are like kindling that feeds the fire of love. In this silence, unbearable to the "outer" man, the Father speaks to us his incarnate Word, who suffered, died, and rose; in this silence the Spirit of adoption enables us to share in the prayer of Jesus.

2718 Contemplative prayer is a union with the prayer of Christ insofar as it makes us participate in his mystery. The mystery of Christ is celebrated by the Church in the Eucharist, and the Holy Spirit makes it come alive in contemplative prayer so that our charity will manifest it in our acts.

2719 Contemplative prayer is a communion of love bearing life for the multitude, to the extent that it consents to abide in the night of faith. The Paschal night of the Resurrection passes through the night of the agony and the tomb—the three intense moments of the Hour of Jesus which his Spirit (and not "the flesh [which] is weak") brings to life in prayer. We must be willing to "keep watch with (him) one hour".

Exhibit III

The Apostles' and Nicene Creeds

"The Apostles' Creed is so called because it is rightly considered to be a faithful summary of the apostles' faith. It is the ancient baptismal symbol of the Church of Rome. Its great authority arises from this fact: it is 'the Creed of the Roman Church, the See of Peter the first of the apostles, to which he brought the common faith'.

The Niceno-Constantinopolitan or Nicene Creed draws its great authority from the fact that it stems from the first two ecumenical Councils (in 325 and 381). It remains common to all the great churches of both East and West to this day."[1]

These creeds are so central to our faith that the Catholic Catechism uses these as the foundation in explaining our faith, so much that it takes from page 17 to 298 to explain it all! As mentioned before, the Catholic Catechism is a wonderful research document for you to refer to regarding what and why we believe what we believe.

The Apostles' Creed, constitutes, as it were, "the oldest Roman catechism", while the Nicene Creed is more explicit and more detailed.

"As on the day of our Baptism, when our whole life was entrusted to the 'standard of teaching', let us embrace the Creed of our life-giving faith. To say the Credo with faith is to enter into communion with God, Father, Son and Holy Spirit, and also with the whole Church which transmits the faith to us and in whose midst we believe: This Creed is the spiritual seal, our heart's meditation and an ever-present guardian; it is, unquestionably, the treasure of our soul."[2]

The Apostles' Creed

I believe in God the Father almighty, creator of heaven and earth.

I believe in Jesus Christ, his only Son, our Lord.

He was conceived by the power of the Holy Spirit and born of the Virgin Mary

Under Pontius Pilate He was crucified, died, and was buried.

He descended to the dead.

On the third day he rose again.

He ascended into heaven and is seated at the right hand of the Father.

He will come again to judge the living and the dead.

I believe in the Holy Spirit,

the holy catholic Church,

the communion of saints,

the forgiveness of sins,

the resurrection of the body,

and the life everlasting.

Amen.

The Nicene Creed

I believe in one God,

the Father almighty,

maker of heaven and earth,

of all things visible and invisible.

I believe in one Lord Jesus Christ,

the Only Begotten Son of God,

born of the Father before all ages.

God from God, Light from Light,

true God from true God,

begotten, not made, consubstantial with the Father;

through him all things were made.

For us men and for our salvation

he came down from heaven,

and by the Holy Spirit was incarnate of the Virgin Mary,

and became man.

For our sake he was crucified under Pontius Pilate,

he suffered death and was buried,

and rose again on the third day

in accordance with the Scriptures.

He ascended into heaven

and is seated at the right hand of the Father.

He will come again in glory

to judge the living and the dead

and his kingdom will have no end.

I believe in the Holy Spirit, the Lord, the giver of life,

who proceeds from the Father and the Son,

who with the Father and the Son is adored and glorified,

who has spoken through the prophets.

I believe in one, holy, catholic and apostolic Church.

I confess one Baptism for the forgiveness of sins

and I look forward to the resurrection of the dead

and the life of the world to come. Amen.

Exhibit IV

Transubstantiation

What is all of this hocus-pocus? We have all heard this line before. Do you know where it comes from? During the Latin Mass, or our ONLY version of the Mass before Vatican II, during the consecration, the priest raised the host and said, "Hoc est corpus meum," translated as "This is my body." Non-Catholics didn't understand the reverence or the true event happening so they made fun of it.

As Catholics, we believe that the host truly becomes the body of Christ. It is a miracle. In the last chapter we talked about miracles and their frequency. Well, this is mind-blowing, a miracle happens every time a priest calls on Christ to become the body and blood encapsulated in the "accidents" of the physical host and wine. That means there are millions of miracles happening every day!

Let's look at some background here. All four Gospels and Paul's letter to the Corinthians describe the last supper and have Jesus saying the words, "This is my body."

John chapter 6 goes into detail to ensure there is no confusion. 6:51 states, "I am the living bread that came down out of heaven; if anyone eats of this bread, he will live forever; and the bread also which I will give for the life of the world is My flesh."

Scripture scholars attest that the Greek word used for eat, trogo, is more accurately translated as gnaw or chew. Jesus is being very specific here.

The passage continues: "The Jews quarreled among themselves, saying, 'How can this man give us [his] flesh to eat?'

Jesus said to them, 'Amen, amen, I say to you, unless you eat the flesh of the Son of Man and drink his blood, you do not have life within you. Whoever eats my flesh and drinks my blood has eternal life, and I will raise him on the last day. For my flesh is true food, and my blood is true drink. Whoever eats my flesh and drinks my blood remains in me and I in him. Just as the living Father sent me and I have life because of the Father, so also the one who feeds on me will have life because of me.'"

So, not only does Jesus tell his followers to eat his flesh, after the Jews push back, Jesus doubles down. If Jesus was speaking metaphorically, the Jews would not be so aghast. They obviously know what he is saying. And then, just to make sure there is no question as to the significance of his statements at the time, the author goes on:

"Then many of his disciples who were listening said, 'This saying is hard; who can accept it?'

Since Jesus knew that his disciples were murmuring about this, he said to them, 'Does this shock you?' As a result of this, many [of] his disciples returned to their former way of life and no longer accompanied him. Jesus then said to the Twelve, 'Do you also want to leave?'

Simon Peter answered him, 'Master, to whom shall we go? You have the words of eternal life.'" [1]

It is ironic that a minister who claims, "Sola scriptura", that is, solely through scripture, would say, "no, Jesus did not mean this literally." It is pretty clear. Why else would people leave?

Yet, this concept is challenging for us today. We have to believe that God transforms Himself each and every time the priest calls upon Him. Like in the past, "this saying is hard."

Many Catholics, or those who consider converting to be a Catholic, struggle with this saying. Some of us go through a very detailed logical analysis and end up unsettled. Others pray for understanding. Still others just decide to believe. For me, it came down to this. After years of on again, off again questioning, I finally concluded that, "hey, if God does perform miracles, and many of them involve physical changes such as curing of leprosy or other illnesses, why would something where the physical remains the same ("the accidents") but the spiritual goes through a miraculous change be harder to believe? And so, with faith, I chose to believe.

For more information and understanding of this core belief go to the Catholic Catechism 1373-1377,1413

Exhibit V

A Detailed Catholic Examination of Conscience

Here is an example of detailed examination of conscience. (Author unknown but published repeatedly).

A good Catholic examination of conscience can be a great help in making a new start in the life of faith. We use an examination of conscience to help call to mind our sins and failings during a period of quiet reflection before approaching the priest in Confession. It's important for a good Catholic examination of conscience to be thorough. This will help you learn about things that you may not be aware of. It's also a chance to develop your conscience. This is a critical aid for the beginning Catholic.

To make an examination:

- Set aside some quiet time for reflection.
- Start by praying to the Holy Spirit, asking for help in making a good examination to prepare for Confession.
- Read through the items on this list and honestly reflect on your behavior for each item.
- If necessary, take this list or some brief notes (keep them private!) to Confession to help you remember things.

A Catholic examination of conscience traditionally follows the outline of the Ten Commandments and the Precepts of the Catholic Church.

The Ten Commandments

First Commandment

I am the LORD your God.

You shall worship the Lord your God and Him only shall you serve.

Have I...

- Disobeyed the commandments of God or the Church?
- Refused to accept what God has revealed as true, or what the Catholic Church proposes for belief?
- Denied the existence of God?
- Nourished and protected my faith?
- Rejected everything opposed to a sound faith?
- Deliberately misled others about doctrine or the faith?
- Rejected the Catholic faith, joined another Christian denomination, or joined or practiced another religion?
- Joined a group forbidden to Catholics? (Masons, communists, etc.)
- Despaired about my salvation or the forgiveness of my sins?
- Presumed on God's mercy? (Committing a sin in expectation of forgiveness, or asking for forgiveness without conversion and practicing virtue.)
- Loved someone or something more than God? (money, power, sex, ambition, etc.)
- Let someone or something influence my choices more than God?
- Engaged in superstitious practices? (Including horoscopes, fortune tellers, etc.)
- Been involved in the occult? (Seances, Ouija board, worship of Satan, etc.)
- Formally left the Catholic Church?
- Hidden a serious sin or told a lie in confession?

Second Commandment

You shall not take the name of the Lord your God in vain.

Have I...

- Used the name of God in cursing or blasphemy?
- Failed to keep vows or promises that I have made to God?

- Spoken about the Faith, the Church, the saints, or sacred things with irreverence, hatred or defiance?
- Watched television or movies, or listened to music that treated God, the Church, the saints, or sacred things irreverently?
- Used vulgar, suggestive or obscene speech?
- Belittled others in my speech?
- Behaved disrespectfully in Church?
- Misused places or things set apart for the worship of God?
- Committed perjury? (Breaking an oath or lying under oath.)
- Blamed God for my failings?

Third Commandment

Remember to keep holy the Sabbath day.

Have I...

- Set time aside each day for personal prayer to God?
- Missed Mass on Sunday or Holy Days (through own fault without sufficient reason)?
- Committed a sacrilege against the Blessed Sacrament?
- Received a sacrament while in the state of mortal sin?
- Habitually come late to and/or leave early from Mass without a good reason?
- Shop, labor, or do business unnecessarily on Sunday or other Holy Days of Obligation?
- Not taken my children to Mass?
- Knowingly eat meat on a forbidden day (or not fasting on a fast day)?
- Eat or drink within one hour of receiving Communion (other than medical need)?

Fourth Commandment

Honor your father and your mother.

Have I...

- If still under my parents' care, obeyed all that my parents reasonably asked of me?
- Neglected the needs of my parents in their old age or in their time of need?
- If still in school, obeyed the reasonable demands of my teachers?
- Neglected to give my children proper food, clothing, shelter, education, discipline and care (even after Confirmation)?
- Provided for the religious education and formation of my children for as long as they are in my care?
- Ensured that my children still in my care regularly frequent the sacraments of Penance and Holy Communion?
- Educated my children in a way that corresponds to my religious convictions?
- Provided my children with a positive, prudent and personalized education in the Catholic teachings about human sexuality?
- Been to my children a good example of how to live the Catholic Faith?
- Prayed with and for my children?
- Lived in humble obedience to those who legitimately exercise authority over me?
- Broken the law?
- Supported or voted for a politician whose positions are opposed to the teachings of Christ and the Catholic Church?

Fifth Commandment

You shall not kill.

Have I...

- Unjustly and intentionally killed a human being?
- Been involved in an abortion, directly or indirectly? (Such as through advice)
- Seriously considered or attempted suicide?

- Supported, promoted or encouraged the practice of assisted suicide or mercy killing?
- Deliberately desired to kill an innocent human being?
- Unjustly inflicted bodily harm an another person?
- Unjustly threatened another person with bodily harm?
- Verbally or emotionally abused another person?
- Hated another person, or wished him evil?
- Been prejudiced, or unjustly discriminated against others because of their race, color, nationality, sex or religion?
- Joined a hate group?
- Purposely provoked another by teasing or nagging?
- Recklessly endangered my life or health, or that of another, by my actions?
- Driven recklessly or under the influence of alcohol or other drugs?
- Abused alcohol or other drugs?
- Sold or given drugs to others to use for non-therapeutic purposes?
- Used tobacco immoderately?
- Over-eaten?
- Encouraged others to sin by giving scandal?
- Helped another to commit a mortal sin? Through advice or facilitation)
- Caused serious injury or death by criminal neglect?
- Indulged in serious anger?
- Refused to control my temper?
- Been mean to, quarreled with, or willfully hurt someone?
- Been unforgiving to others, when mercy or pardon was requested?
- Sought revenge or hoped something bad would happen to someone?
- Delighted to see someone else get hurt or suffer?
- Treated animals cruelly, causing them to suffer or die needlessly?

Sixth and Ninth Commandments

You shall not commit adultery. You shall not covet your neighbor's wife.

Have I...

- Practiced the virtue of chastity?
- Given in to lust? (The desire for sexual pleasure unrelated to spousal love in marriage.)
- Used an artificial means of birth control?
- Refused to be open to conception, without just cause? (Catechism, 2368)
- Participated in immoral techniques for in vitro fertilization or artificial insemination?
- Sterilized my sex organs for contraceptive purposes?
- Deprived my spouse of the marital right, without just cause?
- Claimed my own marital right without concern for my spouse?
- Deliberately caused male climax outside of normal sexual intercourse? (Catechism, 2366)
- Willfully entertained impure thoughts?
- Purchased, viewed, or made use of pornography?
- Watched movies and television that involve sex and nudity?
- Listened to music or jokes that are harmful to purity?
- Committed adultery? (Sexual relations with someone who is married, or with someone other than my spouse.)
- Committed incest? (Sexual relations with a relative or in-law.)
- Committed fornication? (Sexual relations with someone of the opposite sex when neither of us is married.)
- Engaged in homosexual activity? (Sexual activity with someone of the same sex.)
- Committed rape?
- Masturbated? (Deliberate stimulation of one's own sexual organs for sexual pleasure.)
- Engaged in sexual foreplay (petting) reserved for marriage?
- Preyed upon children or youth for my sexual pleasure?
- Engaged in unnatural sexual activities?
- Engaged in prostitution, or paid for the services of a prostitute?
- Seduced someone, or allowed myself to be seduced?

- Made uninvited and unwelcome sexual advances toward another?
- Purposely dressed immodestly?

Seventh and Tenth Commandments

You shall not steal. You shall not covet your neighbor's goods.

Have I...

- Stolen? (Take something that doesn't belong to me against the reasonable will of
- the owner.)
- Envied others on account of their possessions?
- Tried to live in a spirit of Gospel poverty and simplicity?
- Given generously to others in need?
- Considered that God has provided me with money so that I might use it to benefit others, as well as for my own legitimate needs?
- Freed myself from a consumer mentality?
- Practiced the works of mercy?
- Deliberately defaced, destroyed or lost another's property?
- Cheated on a test, taxes, sports, games, or in business?
- Squandered money in compulsive gambling?
- Made a false claim to an insurance company?
- Paid my employees a living wage, or failed to give a full day's work for a full day's pay?
- Failed to honor my part of a contract?
- Failed to make good on a debt?
- Overcharge someone, especially to take advantage of another's hardship or ignorance?
- Misused natural resources?
- Lied?

Eighth Commandment

You shall not bear false witness against your neighbor.

Have I…

- Knowingly and willfully deceived another?
- Perjured myself under oath?
- Gossiped?
- Committed detraction? (Destroying a person's reputation by telling others about his faults for no good reason.)
- Committed slander or calumny? (Telling lies about another person in order to
- destroy his reputation.)
- Committed libel? (Writing lies about another person in order to destroy his reputation.)
- Been guilty of rash judgment? (Assuming the worst of another person based on circumstantial evidence.)
- Failed to make reparation for a lie I told, or for harm done to a person's reputation?
- Failed to speak out in defense of the Catholic Faith, the Church, or of another person?
- Betrayed another's confidence through speech?

Exhibit VI

My Top 50 Catholic Books (roughly in order)

1. The Catholic Bible
2. The Catechism of The Catholic Church
3. Adolphe Tanquerey "Spiritual Life"
4. John Bartenek, LC "The Better Half"
5. Thomas Kempis "The Imitation of Christ"
6. St. Therese "The Story of a Soul"
7. Ralph Martin "The Fulfillment of all Desire"
8. St. Frances de Sales "Intro to a Devout Life"
9. C.S. Lewis "The Screwtape Letters"*
10. Fr. Walter Ciszek "He Leadth Me"
11. St. Augustine "Confessions"
12. Jacques Philippe "Interior Freedom"
13. Sarah Young, "Jesus Calling"
14. Jean-Baptiste Chautard "The Soul of the Apostolate"
15. Jean Pierre d I I ie Caussade "Abandonment for Divine Providence"
16. Lorenzo Scupoli "Spiritual Combat"
17. Bishop Robert Barron "Thomas Aquinas"
18. Anthony De Mello "Awareness"
19. Rod Bennett "Four Witnesses"
20. Art and Laraine Bennet "The Temperament that God Gave You"
21. Scott Hahn "The Lamb's Supper"
22. Eugene Boylan "This Tremendous Lover"
23. Pope St. John Paul II, "Fides et Ratio"
24. Blessed Columba Marmion "Union with God"
25. Pope St. John Paul II "Crossing the Threshold of Life"
26. Thomas Duboy "Fire Within"
27. St. Alphonse De Liguori "Uniformity with God's Will"
28. C.S. Lewis "The Four Loves"*
29. Cardinal Ratzinger "The Spirit of the Liturgy"

30. Matthew Kelly "Rediscover Catholicism"
31. Archbishop Timothy Dolan "To Whom Shall We Go"
32. Thomas Merton "The Seven Story Mountain"
33. Victor Frankl "Mans Search for Meaning"
34. Blaise Pascal "Penses"
35. St. Theresa of Avila "Interior Castle"
36. Fr. Raoul Plus, S.J. "Progress in Divine Union"
37. St John of the Cross "The Dark Night of the Soul"
38. Fr. John Neuhaus "The Courage to be Catholic"
39. Cardinal Avery Dulles, SJ, "Magisterium"
40. Michael Novak, "Business as a Calling"
41. C.S. Lewis, Reflections on Psalms"*
42. Henry T. Blackaby, "Experiencing God"*
43. Bob Buford, "Half Time"*
44. Patrick M. Morley, "The Man in the Mirror"*
45. Jean Danielou, "God and the Ways of Knowing"
46. Phillip St. Romain, "Pathways to Serenity"
47. G.K. Chesterson, "Orthodoxy"
48. Henri JM Nouwen, "The Return of the Prodigal Son"
49. Matthew Kelly, "The Rhythm of Life"
50. Dr. Henry Cloud, "How People Grow"*

* not a Catholic author